ENCYCLOPEDIA OF THE
Animal World

Vol 4   Bumble bees—Chimpanzee

Bay Books Sydney

A bumblebee on clover with its pollen baskets (the yellow protruberance on each hindleg) filled.

BUMBLEBEES or humblebees, large, furry social bees, living in underground colonies founded by the mother or queen and containing her offspring, the sexually undeveloped females or workers. The queens are produced in the late summer. They hibernate and awake in the spring to begin feeding on the nectar of fruit trees until their ovaries develop. Each queen then searches for a nest-site which is frequently the disused burrow of a small mammal. Depending on the species, the site chosen will be approached by a long tunnel or may be on the surface of the ground but protected by tussocks of grass or moss. Within the nest, the queen prepares a small chamber lined with dried grass and moss and makes a shallow cup or egg-cell from the wax she produces in thin sheets from glands situated between the segments of her abdomen. At this time, the queen begins foraging for pollen which she stores in the egg-cell until there is sufficient to feed her first offspring. 8–14 eggs are laid on the pollen in the cell which is then sealed with a canopy of wax. Once the eggs have been laid, the queen makes a wax honeypot in which she stores some of the nectar she has collected and from which she feeds the growing larvae. This she does by making a hole in the egg-cell and regurgitating the honey from her stomach into the cell.

When the maggot-like larvae have completed their feeding and are full-grown, they spin silken cocoons within which they change into the adult form (pupation). After the young workers chew their way out, the vacated cocoon is used to store honey and pollen. The workers, the ovaries of which normally remain undeveloped, take over the foraging duties of the colony while the queen remains within the nest, making egg-cells on top of the cocoons, laying eggs and in-

cubating them by stretching herself over them like a broody hen.

When the colony is mature, the number of workers may vary from 100–400, although over 2,000 have been recorded in some tropical species. The considerable variation in size of workers results in a division of labour, with the larger bees performing the foraging duties and the smaller ones, or house-bees, restricting themselves to duties within the nest. Among the workers a dominance order is established in which dominant bees (often egg-layers at the time of colony maturity) behave aggressively towards more subordinate bees immediately below them in the social hierarchy, thereby creating a well-regulated social harmony within the colony.

When the colony is mature, the new queens and males are produced. At this time the worker population is at its peak and the number of larvae being produced is relatively small, enabling them to be fed under optimum conditions. The young queens can be distinguished from workers because they build up large fat-body deposits in the abdomen which enable them to survive their hibernation.

After the mating of young queens and their departure for winter quarters, the colony finally disintegrates and its members die off before the winter comes. FAMILY: Bombidae, ORDER: Hymenoptera, CLASS: Insecta, PHYLUM: Arthropoda.   J.P.S.

BUMBLEBEE FISH *Brachygobius xanthozona*, 1¾ in (4 cm) long, a brightly coloured brackish water goby from Sumatra and Borneo. In the wild, it lives in estuaries clinging to wracks with its sucker-like pelvic fins. This species is well known in Europe and the United States because it is com-

monly imported as an aquarium fish. It thrives much better if a little sea salt is added to the water. It is prettily marked with vertical bands of yellow and black but is something of a liability in a community tank since it is an inveterate fin-nipper and will sometimes eat young fishes. FAMILY: Gobidae, ORDER: Perciformes, CLASS: Pisces.

BUNTINGS, the popular name for various groups of relatively small, finch-like birds, in particular the Old World representatives of the subfamily Emberizinae, which some authorities regard as a subdivision of the family Emberizidae which includes tanagers and honeycreepers. Other authorities do not recognize the Emberizidae as a distinct family and have split it up, placing the Emberizinae in the large finch family, the Fringillidae.

The three terms 'bunting', 'finch' and 'sparrow', which are in everday use, are of little taxonomic value since they have been applied so widely and indiscriminately. For instance, while Old World genera of the Emberizinae (e.g. *Emberiza*) are usually called 'buntings', the more numerous New World genera are generally known as 'sparrows' or 'finches' and the name 'bunting' is applied to genera in other groups, for example to some members of the related subfamily Pyrrhuloxiinae (=Richmondeninae), which includes the cardinals. The 'sparrows' of the Old World resemble buntings only superficially and are quite unrelated, most of them being closely related to the African weavers, although one familiar exception is the European 'Hedge sparrow' or dunnock *Prunella modularis*.

Structurally, the emberizine buntings and their allies are alike, mostly being 6 in (15 cm) or less in length, although some may reach 8 in (20 cm). Their bills, which cope with a mainly seed diet, are generally short, conical and attenuated. Some *Emberiza* species possess a distinctive bony knob on the palate for crushing the seeds. The legs are of medium length, while the feet tend to be rather large, being used to scratch for food in ground debris. The tail is often quite long, and in some is graduated or forked, frequently with the outer tail feathers partly or wholly white. Generally, the plumage is streaked or patterned in tones of brown, grey or olive, variously combined with bolder markings of black, white, yellow, green or chestnut. Although often bright, the emberizine buntings are never so brilliantly coloured as some of the related pyrrhuloxine buntings, such as the Indigo bunting *Passerina cyanea* and the Painted bunting *P. ciris* of North America. The males differ from the females in having a black head and bill and a contrasting white nape, moustachial stripe and breast.

The emberizine buntings occur in virtually

all climatic zones of the world from the high Arctic through temperate climates to the tropics. There are some 40 species of Old World buntings, most of which belong to the genus *Emberiza*. The exceptions are the Snow bunting *Plectrophenax nivalis* and the Lapland bunting (or longspur) *Calcarius lapponicus*, both with a circumpolar distribution, and the distinctive Crested bunting *Melophus lathani*, the only representative in tropical and sub-tropical Asia. The numerous *Emberiza* species are predominantly palearctic, although seven occur in Africa and the Rustic bunting *E. rustica* is a vagrant to North America. The genus is now represented in New Zealand following introductions of the Cirl bunting *E. cirlus* and the yellowhammer *E. citrinella* by European settlers a century ago.

The origin of the emberizine buntings is believed to be within the New World where, with around 150 species, the group is most abundant today. The precise relationships within the subfamily and with allied groups, such as the Pyrrhuloxiinae, are difficult to determine. Modern opinion recognizes the need for revision of the present classification of the American emberizines, for their division into over 50 genera, most of which contain only one or two species, hardly seems warranted, even allowing for their diversity. Characteristic of North America are the many genera of 'sparrows', such as *Melospiza*, *Spizella* and *Zonotrichia*, as well as the juncos *Junco* spp and the large and colourful towhees *Pipilo* spp. Other genera are confined to South America, the largest of them being *Atapletes*, comprising numerous species of relatively large and heavily built buntings called Brush finches.

The buntings are predominantly terrestrial, generally occupying relatively open ter-

Indonesian bumblebee fish, imported into the United States and Europe as an aquarium fish.

rain, such as scrubby grasslands and weedy areas, although some occur in denser scrub and woodland. They usually forage on or near to the ground, primarily feeding on seeds, supplemented with other vegetable matter, such as buds, or with small invertebrates, such as insect larvae, the main food of the nestlings. The cup-shaped nest is generally built on or quite near to the ground. From three to seven eggs may be laid, although the clutch is usually of four or five eggs. Most species are multi-brooded. The colouring of the eggs varies, but they usually have a finely spotted or streaked pattern against a lighter background. They are, on the whole, monogamous, although for many years the relatively large Corn bunting *Emberiza calandra* of Europe was believed to be polygamous, at least in some areas. This has recently been questioned by some authorities. Occasional bigamy apparently occurs in certain North American species, such as the Song sparrow *Melospiza melodia* and the White-crowned sparrow *Zonotrichia leucophrys*. A recent study of the Reed bunting *Emberiza schoeniclus* in England has revealed an unusual situation in which individuals quite often change their mate during the course of the season (successive polygamy), while a few males may actually be mated to two or maybe even more females at the same time (harem polygamy). In most respects, however, the life-cycle of the Reed bunting is fairly typical of many other buntings.

Throughout the winter Reed buntings scatter, singly or in small flocks, across open areas of stubble, weedy ground etc., feeding on grain and other seeds. As early as January (in England) the males begin to leave these flocks and arrive at the breeding grounds, staking claims to their territories around suitable areas of marsh or open water. Perching on small bushes or sedges, the males advertise their presence by their rather repetitive song ('tseek-tseek-tesek-tississisk'), successful birds maintaining their ground despite regular, often vociferous, skirmishes with other intruding males, Encouraged by periods of mild weather, this activity is soon suppressed during colder spells when it is necessary to search for more food. The males and some females usually return to the same general area in successive years, the females arriving rather later. As the males become preoccupied with courtship and pair formation, their song intensity declines, usually until nest-building and incubation commences in late April.

In England four to five eggs are usually laid in a cup-shaped nest generally well hidden in ground vegetation. In northern Europe, where more young can apparently be reared due to the longer period of daylight, clutches are regularly of six or seven. The eggs hatch after about 13 days incuba-

tion, The male often assists the female in incubating the eggs and after hatching. Although blind and naked and weighing only about $\frac{1}{12}$ oz (2 gm) when hatched, the young are alert and well feathered by the time they leave the nest 10–12 days later. They do not begin to fly, however, until they are nearly 20 days old, by which time their weight is about $\frac{1}{2}$–$\frac{3}{4}$ oz (17–19 gm). While Reed buntings may successfully rear two broods during the season, most of the repeat clutches are replacements of earlier ones which were lost through predation.

Reed buntings are rather unusual amongst passerine birds in having a very marked distraction display to lure predators away from their nests and young. They feign injury, rustling along the ground with drooped and flapping wings and a widely spread tail, uttering their anxious alarm call 'see'.

By the end of the breeding season, which lasts from late April to August in England, the adult's plumage is very abraded, especially that of the female, and so there is a complete body moult between late June and early November. Continued breeding delays the onset of the moult, which is usually later in the females, for some of them remain in the breeding areas with late broods longer than their respective mates. Individual adults take 50–60 days to moult in Britain. Juveniles also moult in late summer, acquiring their adult plumages by a partial moult, usually confined to the head and body regions and a few areas on the wing.

Following the moult Reed buntings become more gregarious, gathering together at communal roosts in reed-beds overnight and feeding in loose flocks by day. In northern Europe the breeding populations are entirely migratory, wintering in warmer climes to the south, while in Britain the species is only a partial migrant.

In northeast Asia the Reed bunting is replaced by a closely allied species, Pallas's reed bunting *E. pallasi*, although in eastern Siberia the two species breed alongside each other. The song of *pallasi* is faster and higher-pitched than *schoeniclus*, more like the Ortolan bunting *E. hortulana*, while the upperparts are noticeably paler and the nape of the male is pale yellow, not white. Undoubtedly the two species originated from the same ancestral stock through geographical isolation. A similar pair consists of the Ortolan and Cretzschmar's bunting *E. caesia*. Both look very much alike, *hortulana* being widely distributed in open hilly country throughout much of the western Palearctic (but not Britain), while *caesia* only breeds in rocky and semi-arid regions in parts of the eastern Mediterranean.

Many buntings occur in subspecific forms or races, but often the distinctions are not immediately obvious until the various types

Male reed bunting at the nest. This bunting inhabits damp ground, not only reed-beds, and tends to come to bird tables in western European gardens.

are critically compared in the hand. Thus, while yellowhammers in south and east Britain are typical of the Continental race, *citrinella,* the plumage gradually becomes a little darker, more richly coloured and more heavily streaked to the north and west, grading into the race *caliginosa.* Together with the Corn bunting, the yellowhammer is a familiar species of arable areas throughout Europe, the bright lemon yellow head and underparts of the male being just as distinctive as its song, popularly rendered as 'a-little-bit-of-bread-and-no-cheese'. In eastern and central Asia the yellowhammer is replaced by the Pine bunting, which many authorities regard as a separate species, *E. leucocephalos,* although from central and western Siberia a large number of specimens with intermediate plumage are known, indicating that the two forms are 'strong' subspecies which hybridize extensively in the area of overlap. The Pine bunting lacks yellow colouration in its plumage, the male's head being boldly patterned in white and chestnut. Its preferred habitat is wooded or bushy steppe. In the Mediterranean climatic zone of Europe the Cirl bunting *E. cirlus*

replaces the yellowhammer. The male can readily be distinguished from the male yellowhammer by its bold black and yellow face-pattern and with practice by its more hurried, jingled song, which lacks the terminal 'cheese' phrase of the yellowhammer. But the two species are nevertheless very similar, and have probably also diverged from the same stock through geographical isolation. In Britain, where both species occur, *cirlus* is distinctly local and confined to the southern counties, while *citrinella* is widespread.

The Black-headed bunting of the eastern Mediterranean and Iran and the Red-headed bunting of Turkestan are two colourful *Emberiza* currently regarded as two 'strong' races of *E. melanocephala,* although formerly they were thought to be distinct species (*E. melanocephala* and *E. bruniceps* respectively). Birds of intermediate plumage have been located in a small area of overlap, indicating that the two types are able to hybridize. True species do not interbreed. See also American buntings and Song sparrows. FAMILY: Emberizidae, ORDER: Passeriformes, CLASS: Aves   B.D.B.

BUOYANCY. The specific gravity of most animal tissue is greater than that of both fresh and salt water, though where the salt concentration of water is unusually high animals may float. People who have swum in the very salt water of the Dead Sea know that it requires no effort to float on the surface. So aquatic animals will usually sink unless they use energy to maintain their position or in some way alter their density so that they are buoyant. Such buoyancy can be attained in three main ways: by increasing the ratio of surface area to volume; by including in the body lighter materials; or by excluding the heavier elements in the body fluids. All of these methods are employed by marine animals.

The bodies of the animals and plants which form the plankton often are decorated with long spines or arms. These serve to increase the surface area of the body without adding much weight and therefore the organism will not only sink more slowly but the slightest movement in the water will take it upwards.

The use by planktonic animals of spines for flotation is reinforced by the inclusion in their bodies of oil droplets and fat deposits.

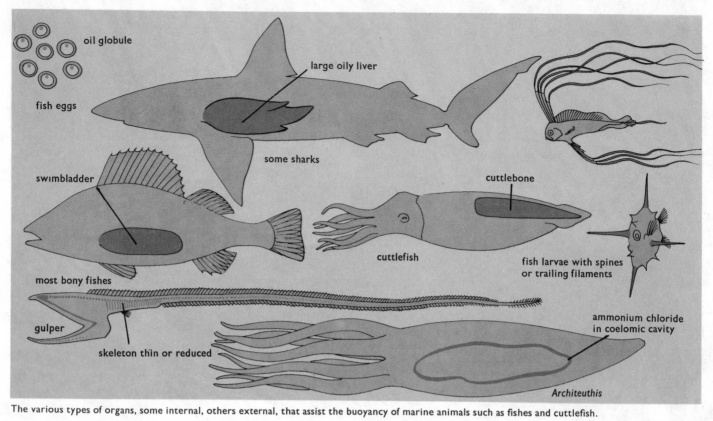

The various types of organs, some internal, others external, that assist the buoyancy of marine animals such as fishes and cuttlefish.

These are particularly important in fish eggs that are pelagic. In adult fishes, too, fats are important. The large livers of sharks make up about 25% of their body volume and are packed with squalene, a hydrocarbon with a specific gravity of 0·86 (giving it 70% greater lifting power than other fish oils). This is their main method of attaining buoyancy.

The air-bladders of many bony fishes play an important part in buoyancy. Those like the salmon whose air-bladder opens to the outside through the oesophagus can regulate the amount of gas contained in it. They gulp air at the surface to increase bouyancy or release bubbles from the bladder to sink. But many fishes have closed bladders and in these gas can be secreted into the bladder from the blood or absorbed from it at need. See swimbladder.

Bathypelagic squids often reach very large sizes. For example *Architeuthis* may be 50 ft (15 m) in total length. These very large animals remain buoyant because their coelomic cavity is filled with a low specific gravity liquid, a solution of ammonium chloride. Pressure has little effect on the volume as water is virtually incompressible, therefore this is effective at all depths. If a squid, such as *Cranchia,* is drained of this fluid it sinks.

The cuttlefish, on the other hand, has an efficient buoyancy mechanism in its cuttlebone, which is divided into numerous tiny chambers so arranged that the whole structure is very strong and can withstand great pressures. The chambers contain nitrogen, the remainder of the space being filled with water containing salts. If the salt concentration is high, water is drawn by *osmosis from the rest of the body; if low, water moves out. An ion pump or salt extractor controls this level. The result of water being drawn in or pumped out is that the density of cuttlebone varies from about 0·5 (containing 10% liquid) to almost 0·7 (containing 30% liquid). At 0·6 an animal weighing 2·2 lb (1 kg) develops an upthrust of 0·09 lb (40 gm) which will just about balance the excess weight in the sea water. That is, it is adjusted for neutral buoyancy, which means it will float at any chosen depth because its specific gravity is that of the surrounding fluid.   J.D.C.

Burbot, the only freshwater cod.

BURBOT *Lota lota,* the only freshwater member of the cod family. It derives its common name from the Latin for a beard, a reference to the barbel on its chin. The burbot lives in most European rivers except those in the extreme north and south. Its nearest relative is the ling. It has an elongated, subcylindrical body blotched with shades of brown and its general form has given rise to an alternative name, eelpout. It was formerly found in most eastward-flowing rivers in England and its great stronghold was the Norfolk Broads. In recent times a variety of factors such as draining the land and other works have led to the burbot becoming very rare in England and for several years there have been no reliable reports of specimens having been caught. A rather secretive fish, it lurks near the bottom among weeds during the day but comes out at night to feed on frogs and small fishes. The burbot is also found in Asia and there are two subspecies in North America. It usually grows to 24 in (60 cm) but sometimes to as much as 39 in (98 cm). FAMILY: Gadidae, ORDER: Gadiformes, CLASS: Pisces.

BURYING BEETLES, also known as Sexton beetles, are famous for burying the corpses of small birds and mammals, on which they lay their eggs, the larvae from these feeding on the decaying flesh. See Carrion beetles.

BUSH-BABIES, nocturnal mammals with forward-pointing eyes and grasping hands and feet. The name is based upon the soft, woolly fur and the large, staring eyes. The Common bush-baby *Galago senegalensis*, which weighs just over 1 lb (500 gm), with head and body 17 in (42 cm) and tail 10 in (25 cm) long, is the best known and is often found in captivity in Europe and America. It has grey or greyish-brown fur and the long tail is very bushy. The smallest of this group is the Dwarf bush-baby *Galago demidovii*, which in weight, size and general habits, is very reminiscent of the Mouse lemur of Madagascar. It weighs only 2 oz (60 gm); the head and body together measure only 6 in (15 cm), and the tail is 8 in (20 cm) long. The fur is a dark, rufous brown and the pointed snout is very conspicuous. At the other end of the scale, there is the large Thick-tailed bush-baby *Galago crassicaudatus*. With a head and body length of 13 in (33 cm) and a tail 18 in (45 cm) long, it is almost the size of a rabbit. There are also two less well known species, which are about the same size as the Common bush-baby. One is Allen's bush-baby *Galago alleni* and the other is the Needle-clawed bush-baby *Galago elegantulus*. The latter has a claw-like extension in the middle of every nail except those on the thumb and big toe whereas all other bush-babies have flat nails. The thumb and big toe are opposable in all species of bush-baby and are very important in grasping the fine

Baby Thick-tailed bush-baby in nest.

Burying beetle *Necrophorus humator* on carcass of Pygmy shrew.

branches and trunks among which these animals live.

Bush-babies are confined to Africa and there is a distinction between rain-forest forms and steppe and savannah forms. The Dwarf, Allen's and Needle-clawed bush-babies are rain-forest forms with dark brown fur and yellowish-brown underparts. They occur in central West Africa and may also extend into tropical deciduous forest in this area. On the other hand, the Common and Thick-tailed bush-babies occur in steppe and savannah in Central and Southern Africa and have a more greyish fur. In general, these drier area forms are easier to keep in captivity.

Bush-babies are omnivorous. Insects form the major part of the diet, with various other items of animal food and plant food such as fruits, gum and leaves making up the balance. However, each species has its own speciality. The Dwarf bush-baby is a specialized insectivorous form, its diet being about 80% insects. The Needle-clawed bush-baby eats about 90% gum and makes up the rest of its diet entirely with insect food. This specialized diet may explain the presence of the claw-like extension of the nails, since this bush-baby hangs upside down high up in the trees, rather like a European squirrel, to eat the gum. The Common, Allen's and Thick-tailed bush-babies have a fairly mixed animal and plant diet, but each has its special preferences. The

Common bush-baby seems to rely fairly heavily on insects, while the Thick-tailed bush-baby eats larger animal prey and more plant food. All of these specialities are reflected in the teeth. For example, the Thick-tailed bush-baby has stout canines for killing larger animals and flat cusps on the cheek teeth (premolars and molars) for grinding fruit, whereas the Dwarf bush-baby has sharp, pointed canines for stabbing insects and sharp cheek teeth cusps for chewing them.

Every member of the bush-baby group is completely arboreal. The hands and feet grasp the branches with the opposable digits and special adhesive pads on the hands and feet. Jumping is typically vertical, the bush-babies clinging to branches in a vertical position and taking off and landing in this posture. They therefore differ greatly from their nearest relatives, the lorises, angwantibo and pottos, which are very slow-moving mammals with a deliberate, grasping gait. In association with their special manner of clinging and jumping, the bush-babies have elongated back legs, due to the lengthening of the calcaneum and navicular bones.

Most, if not all, bush-babies can build spherical leaf-nests but some species also live in hollow trees. Again there is specialization: the Thick-tailed bush-baby appears to live most often in tree hollows, while the Dwarf bush-baby lives exclusively in rounded leaf-nests. In the species which construct leaf-nests, the nest is usually only occupied for 2–3 weeks; a new one is then constructed. The nest naturally acts as a centre for the home range, and bush-babies apparently defend a territory around their nest. The basic social system common to all bush-babies is that of a bunch of more-or-less overlapping male and female home ranges, but in some species, such as the Dwarf bush-baby and Common bush-baby, small social groups of up to eight individuals are formed, with each social group occupying a common nest. Allen's, Thick-tailed, and Needle-clawed bush-babies, on the other hand, are solitary or live in pairs.

Social grooming of the head of a partner is observed in aggregations of adults, so it seems that social bonds are quite well established between individuals in a group. There are also high-pitched calls which serve to keep the members of a group together. Fighting between the members of a social group of adults is rare and members of a group are often seen feeding in the same tree.

Typically, the female bush-baby gives birth to a single offspring but the Dwarf bush-baby and the Common bush-baby often give birth to twins. However, it is rare for both babies to survive. Unlike the closely related pottos, angwantibos and lorises, bush-babies do not carry their babies on their fur from birth onwards. Instead, the babies are left in a nest when the mother goes off to feed. Thus, the mother sleeps with her baby in the nest during the daytime and then leaves it alone when she is feeding at night. If the nest is disturbed, the mother will usually carry her baby to another nest. This is done by picking it up in the mouth, as in carnivores and rodents. The same type of carriage in the mouth is also seen with the Mouse lemur. Most bush-babies do not have a restricted breeding season, but there may be an annual cycle in the frequency of births. In really dry steppe areas, such as those inhabited by *Galago senegalensis* in parts of its range, there may be two well-defined annual peaks in births. Gestation, generally takes about four months, though it may take as long as five months in the Thick-tailed bush-baby. The baby grows slowly and there is a long period of maternal care. In order to keep the nest clean, the mother licks away the urine and faeces of her offspring.

Bush-babies are distant relatives of man and are placed with lemurs, monkeys, apes and man in the order Primates. They differ quite markedly, along with the loris group and the Madagascar lemurs, from the monkeys, apes and man, so they are placed in the separate suborder Prosimii. They share certain characters with the lorises, angwantibos, pottos and lemurs which indicate that they had a common ancestor distinct from that which gave rise to the living monkeys and apes. The major characters of the Prosimii are: the presence of a 'tooth-comb' in the lower jaw which is formed from the horizontal incisors and canines, the possession of a 'toilet-claw' on the second toe of each foot, a special (epitheliochorial) type of placentation, the absence of a bony wall behind the eye and the simple structure of the uterus. FAMILY: Galagidae, ORDER: Primates, CLASS: Mammalia.   R.D.M.

BUSH-BABY POLLINATION, occasionally flowers are pollinated by larger animals than insects. Fruit bats and nectar-eating birds are known to transfer pollen on their heads from flower to flower and in 1964 it was suggested that Thick-tailed bush-babies sometimes pollinated the flowers of Baobab trees. Although they ate parts of the flowers they left the pistils undamaged and, as the bush-babies could be seen to have their faces covered in pollen, pollination must almost certainly have taken place.

BUSHBUCK *Tragelaphus scriptus,* red-coated antelope with a variable number of white stripes and spots on the flanks. Also known in some areas as the Harnessed antelope, it is related to the *kudu and is found over most of Africa south of the Sahara.

BUSH-CRICKETS, jumping insects of moderate to large size closely related to the crickets and also known as 'katydids' or 'Long-horned grasshoppers'. The antennae are thread-like, longer than the body and composed of more than 30 segments. Behind the head is a saddle-shaped structure, the pronotum, protecting the front part of the thorax. There are usually two pairs of fully developed wings, but these may be reduced in size or completely absent. The hindwings are membranous and fold up like a fan beneath the tougher forewings when at rest. The hindlegs are usually much enlarged for jumping, but the attachments of the jumping muscles do not form the herring-bone pattern on the hind femora found in the grasshoppers, which are superficially similar in appearance. The females usually have a conspicuous egg-laying structure or ovipositor at the tip of the abdomen.

There are about 4,000 species and the distribution is world-wide, and although the group is mainly tropical there are many temperate species.

The eggs are sometimes laid in the ground, but more often in or on the stems or leaves of plants. They are often laid in groups but never in a pod as in grasshoppers. The young are usually similar to the adults in appearance, though lacking wings, and reach maturity after moulting between five and ten or more times during a period varying from a few weeks to several months.

Almost all male bush-crickets can produce sounds by rubbing the hind edge of the right forewing against a row of teeth on the left forewing. These 'songs' are high-pitched and often mainly ultrasonic, but most contain sounds that are audible to the human ear and some are quite deafening. In some species

The Common bush-baby *Galago senegalensis* has many names, such as Moholi galago, Senegal galago and night-ape. It is nocturnal and cries like a baby, hence its name. Despite this it has been a popular pet for the last 20 years.

Female bushbuck or Harnessed antelope, of Africa.

Face of Giant West Indian bush-cricket *Nesonotus denticulatus.*

large numbers of insects are able to synchronize their songs with one another with extraordinary precision. The females are usually silent, but both sexes have a hearing organ in each foreleg.

Many bush-crickets are leaf-like in appearance and in some the forewings have a remarkably close resemblance to leaves, even to the extent of having marks like those made by leaf-mining insects and the wing-margins cut away as though eaten by caterpillars. Some bush-crickets appear to mimic other insects in their structure and behaviour. The young of some species mimic ants or beetles, while the adults are leaf-like and totally different in appearance.

Although most bush-crickets are harmless to man, the Mormon cricket *Anabrus simplex*

has been a serious pest in the western USA ever since the early settlers began to cultivate the land. When the weather conditions favour an outbreak, the half-grown young of this flightless insect form vast swarms that migrate in bands, rather like locust hoppers, ruining the crops in their path. Another bush-cricket that shows locust-like behaviour is the African form of *Homorocoryphus nitidulus,* the flying adults of which can migrate over distances of several hundred miles and are sometimes sufficiently numerous to damage crops.

Most bush-crickets show a tendency to be nocturnal and some are exclusively so. They vary in feeding habits from entirely carnivorous to entirely vegetarian, but most feed on a mixture of plant and animal matter. FAMILY: Tettigoniidae, ORDER: Orthoptera, CLASS: Insecta, PHYLUM: Arthropoda. D.R.R.

BUSH-CRICKETS. The Mormon cricket that was such a serious pest to early settlers in the western USA got its name from the ravages it caused to the crops of the Mormons when they first settled in Utah. Their crops were on the verge of being destroyed and famine was threatening when flocks of Franklin gulls *Larus pipixcan* descended on the crickets and wiped them out. The Mormons commemorated the event with a monument at Salt Lake City—a tall marble pillar surmounted by a ball with two gulls perched on it. The Franklin gull is unusual in that it lives inland, nesting in marshes, and is sometimes called the 'Prairie pigeon'.

BUSHDOG *Speothos venaticus,* shortlegged, sausage-shaped carnivore in the same family, Canidae, as wild and domestic dogs,

but not a close relative. In addition to its undoglike body shape, it has small ears, a short, almost naked tail, and dark brown fur with a golden ruff. It is adapted in body shape for rapid movement through the dense undergrowth which surrounds the river banks of the tropical forests where it lives. The bushdog is reported to be an excellent swimmer, and its size is well-suited for this. Further features distinguishing it from other dogs are found in the thickness of its bones and in its dentition. The bushdog possesses only 36 teeth compared with the typical canid number of 42.

The bushdog is 22–30 in (57–75 cm) long in head and body with a 5–6 in (12–15 cm) tail, and it is 9–12 in (23–30 cm) at the shoulder. It weighs 12–15 lb (5–7 kg).

Ranging through the tropical forests of Central America and northern South America, bushdogs travel in packs, preying upon large rodents such as pacas and agoutis as well as small forest deer. Fishing is another means of obtaining food. Bushdogs are reputed to be vicious, and the Indians, who refer to them as Warracaba tigers (because their call resembles that of the warracaba or trumpetbird *Psophia crepitans*), 'are said to flee whenever a pack approaches. However, when tamed, they are extremely friendly and playful.

Little is known of their breeding habits in the wild, but females probably dig burrows in which to rear their offspring. In captivity, females come into heat twice a year (in spring and autumn), like the domestic dog, but unlike most wild canids. During heat, a female is very active, patrolling her territory and leaving scent-marks which informs neighbouring males that she is prepared to mate. The scent-marking posture of the female is unique; she climbs up a tree backwards, ending in a handstand, urinates and deposits scent, and then slides down. Males leave scent-marks on bushes, logs, and rocks all year round, lifting the hindleg just as domestic dogs do.

Among themselves, bushdogs are extremely sociable, vigorously wagging their short tails to indicate friendliness. A dominance hierarchy develops among males, and the more subordinate individuals express their status by laying the ears back, lowering the tail, and crouching or turning over onto their backs when approached by a superior. Dominant males hold the body erect and tall, with the tail raised and held stiffly. During fights, bushdogs try to grasp and bite the neck of their opponent; if they get a secure hold, they shake the head, almost as though the victim were prey. However, bushdogs

Plant stem containing eggs of the Green bush-cricket *Conocephalus discolor.*

African bush-cricket, one of several thousand species of crickets with long antennae that inhabit bushes and shrubs, the females laying their eggs in the twigs.

have very thick necks, and this probably prevents them being harmed seriously during fights.

Bushdogs have two vocalizations which are unusual. One call, a high-pitched squeak which sounds like a bird and is heard almost constantly, probably functions to keep pack members in touch with one another in the forest. The second is a piercing screech given by aggressive animals after a fight. FAMILY: Canidae, ORDER: Carnivora, CLASS: Mammalia. D.G.K.

BUSHMASTER *Lachesis muta,* the longest of the New World venomous snakes inhabiting the northern portions of South America, Trinidad and ranging northward into Central America to Costa Rica. Although it does not attain the volume or weight of the largest rattlesnakes, the bushmaster can exceed 12 ft (3·6 m) in length. It is the only egg-laying (oviparous) species of the New World Pit vipers, and apparently the female incubates the eggs.

Large fangs inject considerable venom deep into prey which is usually held fast, whereas most viperine snakes, for reasons of safety, bite and then release their prey, to follow it to where it dies. The tail terminates in an incomplete, silent, small 'rattle.' The bushmaster may be locally plentiful throughout its patchy range but is seldom seen due to its retiring nature. It prefers to remain concealed but if unduly disturbed, it has a lengthy striking reach. This, plus its peculiar manner of striking, may bring it ever closer to the intruder rather than farther away. Bites are, however, not as common with this species as among the fer-de-lance of the same areas. In captivity, the bushmaster is keenly aware of its surroundings and its quiet, almost lethargic appearance is deceptive. FAMILY: Crotalidae, ORDER: Squamata, CLASS: Reptilia.

BUSHPIG *Potamochoerus porcus,* or Water hog or Redriver hog, a large hog with reddish-brown coarse hair over its entire body. Bushpigs are found throughout most of Africa south of the Sahara and in Madagascar.

The male bushpig is larger than the female. Recent research in Rhodesia established that adult males average 50 in (1·25 m) in length as against 47 in (1·19 m) for adult females. Height at the shoulder averaged 30 in (75 cm) for the males and 27 in (68 cm) for the females. Tails ranged from 12·2–17 in (31–43 cm) for the males as against 12–15·5 in (30–39 cm) for the females. It is not surprising that weight differed too, though the smallest adult male weighed less than the smallest female: 144 lb (65 kg) and 155 lb (70 kg) respectively. However, the largest male weighed 250 lb (114 kg), the largest female only 200 lb (91 kg).

During the same research in Rhodesia 92 skulls were examined of which 3 had 44 teeth, 16 had 40, while by far the greater number, 73, had 42 according to the following formula: incisors $\frac{3}{3}$; canines $\frac{1}{1}$; premolars $\frac{3}{3}$ or $\frac{4}{4}$; molars $\frac{3}{3} \times 2$.

The time of year of breeding varies in different parts of Africa, but generally farrowing coincides with the rainy season. In most areas this is from October to March. The gestation period has been reported as four months. The litter size is from two to six usually three or four. Captive females have been known to breed when 86 weeks of age. At birth young are brown with lighter longitudinal stripes. The average weight of five young a few days old was 1·75 lb (800 gm). Young are precocial (able to run soon after birth) and able to travel with the mother when a few days old. The female makes a large nest of grass for the young. These nests, locally called 'bowers' in southern Africa, remain for many months in heavily wooded country and resemble a small haystack.

Bushpigs inhabit brushy woodland and grassy areas. They travel in bands of from 4 to 20. They are almost entirely nocturnal except in remote areas where they move about in daylight if undisturbed. During daytime they seek refuge in the tall grass and bush where they remain until darkness. They eat chiefly roots, bulbs and fruits and are reputed to devour reptiles, birds, eggs and carrion. In agricultural areas surrounded by brushy timber, the bushpig makes domestic crops a large part of its diet. Maize, groundnuts and field peas are heavily damaged by bushpigs.

Because of their fondness for agricultural crops they are constantly hunted by farmers who use dogs and large groups of drivers to force the animals into open country. Even when located the bushpig is not easy to kill and is a formidable adversary. Dogs are often maimed or killed in such encounters. Bushpigs are hosts of trypanosomes which cause sleeping sickness in cattle and are fed upon by the Tsetse fly which carries the trypanosomes to cattle. For this reason the bushpig has been eliminated in some parts of Africa where cattle are reared. FAMILY: Suidae, SUBORDER: Suiformes, ORDER: Artiodactyla, CLASS: Mammalia. L.K.S.

BUSTARDS, a well-defined family of 22 species related to the seriemas, cranes and rails, some being called korhaans in South Africa or floricans in India. They are birds of deserts, grassy plains and open savannahs. They vary in size from about 14 in (35 cm) long in the Lesser florican *Sypheotides indica* of India, to more than 50 in (130 cm) long in the Kori bustard *Ardeotis kori* of Africa. Males are generally larger than females. The Kori bustard and others of the same genus are among the largest and heaviest of all flying birds attaining weights of more than 30 lb (13·5 kg). They are close to the size limit above which flight is impossible and only fly reluctantly and for short distances. Smaller species fly strongly, many performing migrations of considerable length, but even so they depend more upon running and their cryptic colouring to escape predators. All bustards have long, strong legs and a long neck. Their three forward pointing toes are short and broad, while the hind toe, or hallux, is absent

The bushpig *Potamochoerus porcus* is a large hog with coarse hair over its entire body. It is also the commonest wild pig of Africa, but one seldom seen since it is nocturnal and keeps to thick cover. Although omnivorous it often makes domestic crops its diet and is hunted by farmers.

as in many other cursorial species. The plumage is various shades of grey, brown and buff, beautifully vermiculated and spotted with black and white, and other shades of grey and brown. The majority of bustards have large white patches on their wings, which are usually visible only in flight. Several species have short crests, while the males of some, such as the Great bustard *Otis tarda* of Eurasia and the Houbara bustard *Chlamydotis undulata* of northern Africa and southwestern Asia, have ornate bristles or plumes on the head and neck. These plumes are much in evidence in their elaborate terrestrial courtship displays, as are the white patches displayed on their drooping wings. The males of the Kori bustard and Great bustard are described as seeming to turn themselves inside-out as they posture in front of rivals and females, transforming themselves from being dull and inconspicuous to strikingly white. The males of a number of species, such as the Black-bellied bustard *Lissotis melanogaster,* have black underparts. Such males have a beautiful aerial display in which they parachute out of the sky, their black under-parts appearing in vivid contrast to the white of their wings.

Bustards are found mainly in Africa but six species occur in Eurasia and one in Australia. The Great bustard formerly bred in Britain, but became extinct there in about 1832.

Bustards lay their eggs in a scrape on the ground, the clutch varying from one or two in the larger species to five in some of the smaller species.

The female sits very tight while incubating and relies on her cryptic colouring to escape detection. In a few species the male remains with the female during the breeding season, but in others the male is polygamous and the eggs and young are tended by the female alone. The young are nidifugous and hatch covered in down, leaving the nest almost immediately.

Bustards are omnivorous, consuming a great variety of seeds, fruits, insects and small vertebrates. They are considered to be good sport and good eating throughout their range, and have suffered accordingly in populated areas. They also suffer from modern farming methods, particularly in Europe. FAMILY: Otidae, ORDER: Gruiformes, CLASS: Aves.
M.P.L.F.

BUTCHERBIRD, name referring to two distinct families of Passeriformes (suborder Oscines), the true shrikes (Laniidae) and the Australian butcherbirds (Cracticidae). The name derives from their remarkable habit of impaling insects, lizards, birds and mammals on thorns. Prey thus fixed is readily dismembered and a larder formed for times of food scarcity. See also shrike and Australian magpie.

The Great bustard, of Europe and Asia, is vulnerable to guns because of its unwillingness to fly.

BUTTERFISH, or gunnel *Pholis gunnellus,* an elongated blenny-like fish commonly found hiding under stones along European and North American coasts when the tide is out. Generally it is buff-coloured with a row of black spots along the base of the long dorsal fin; the pectoral fin may be orange or yellowish. The body is covered with fine scales and is slimy; anybody trying to pick it up will be in no doubt why it is called the butterfish.

The breeding of this fish is quite unusual. The female lays the eggs in a small clump about 1 in (2·5 cm) in diameter, the eggs being compacted into a ball by the female curving her body into a loop and laying the eggs within the circle. The ball of eggs is then thrust into a hole in the rocks or into an empty shell. Both parents (which is a rare procedure in fishes) take turns in guarding the eggs until the young hatch after about four weeks. The young swim out to sea for several months and then return to the shore. Most fishes have paired ovaries, but in the butterfish there is a single long ovary. These fishes grow to about 10–12 in (25–30 cm) in length. FAMILY: Pholididae, ORDER: Perciformes, CLASS: Pisces.

Butterfish, of the coasts of western Europe, so called for its slippery, slimy skin.

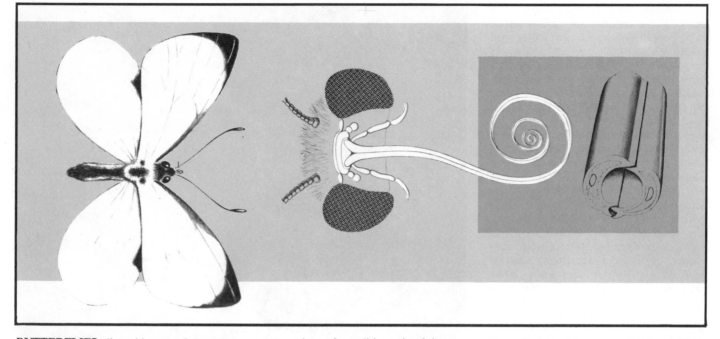

BUTTERFLIES, diurnal insects of the order Lepidoptera, with large, often brightly coloured wings. Their general characteristics are to be found under Lepidoptera and the distinctions between them and moths are described in the article on the latter group. The butterflies of any one country may be either widespread, and therefore adapted to a great variety of conditions, local because closely adjusted to certain environments, or they may be maintained by migration. This may also augment some of the native species, such as the Small tortoiseshell *Aglias urticae* of Britain.

The earlier stages of butterflies are to some extent characteristic, especially the

Butterfly (left) with tongue coiled but visible in front of head. Head enlarged (centre) with tongue uncoiling. Portion of tongue (right) showing tubular structure achieved by folding.

Male Purple emperor butterfly *Apatura iris*.

chrysalis. In moths, this is typically enclosed within a cocoon of silk, frequently subterranean. In butterflies it is generally fully exposed, protected by its colour-pattern. In some of the species, it is attached by the tail and held upright by a silken belt, which appears to be a relic of the cocoon that is so usual in moths. In others, even this has disappeared and the chrysalis hangs head downwards from the tail alone. There are, however, a few instances of concealed and even subterranean butterfly chrysalids. The latter are not derived from the moth situation, but represent a condition acquired independently; for the butterflies are, indeed, a highly specialized group. ORDER: Lepidoptera, CLASS: Insecta, PHYLUM: Arthropoda.   E.B.F.

BUTTERFLYFISHES, a common name used for two quite distinct groups of fishes, an African freshwater flying fish and a group of marine, coral reef fishes of the family Chaetodontidae.

1. Freshwater. The butterflyfish *Pantodon buchholzi,* a species from central West Africa related to the Bony tongues. It has the distinction of being one of the few freshwater flying fishes. Growing to 4 in (10 cm) in length, it has the head and body flattened somewhat on top and rounded below. The back and sides are mottled brown and dark green. The pectoral fins, from which the fish derives its name, are large and are coloured brown and white, while the pelvic fins are reduced to four long finrays ringed alternately with brown and white. The latter are spread like a fan when the fish is cruising gently in water. The central rays of the tail are also elongated.

The flight of the butterflyfish is interesting. The pectoral skeleton is enlarged to allow for the greatly developed muscles that operate the pectoral fins, which are actually flapped in flight (see Flight in fishes). In the wild, this species is found in lakes, ponds and sluggish weedy waters. It feeds on small fishes and also insects which have dropped into the water and is reported to be able to catch insects while it is out of the water. Butterflyfishes can be kept in large and fairly shallow aquaria, which must of course be covered. They need live food and it is advisable to keep a culture of cockroaches or flies for this purpose.

Breeding is also possible in captivity. The male at first holds the female with his elongated pelvic rays but later wraps himself around her. The middle rays of his anal fin are elongated to form a tube so that it is easy to recognize the sexes. The eggs float on the surface of the water and hatch in three days at 86°F (30°C). Very small insects such as greenfly (aphids) should be provided for the young. FAMILY: Pantodontidae, ORDER: Osteoglossiformes, CLASS: Pisces.

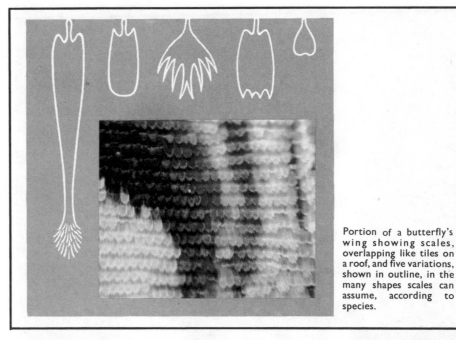

Portion of a butterfly's wing showing scales, overlapping like tiles on a roof, and five variations, shown in outline, in the many shapes scales can assume, according to species.

2. Marine. Small and highly coloured marine fishes belonging to the family Chaetodontidae and found chiefly on coral reefs. They are also known as angelfishes. These butterflyfishes are deep-bodied and compressed with a long dorsal fin (the anterior rays are spiny) and a long anal fin (with the first three rays spiny). The deep body allows for considerable agility and they seem to flutter around coral heads, diving into cracks at the first sign of danger. Often they have a dark vertical bar across the eyes making them inconspicuous and near the tail there is a large eye-spot. It is thought that predators mistake the tail of the fish for the head, an illusion that is encouraged by some

Butterflyfish, a freshwater flying fish, using actual beats of the fins rather than gliding.

Imperial angelfish, one of the marine butterflyfishes noted for their bright colours.

species which on occasion will swim slowly backwards.

The colours of these fishes are often quite splendid and are well shown in the accompanying pictures. In some species, such as the Imperial angelfish *Pomacanthus imperator,* the colouration in the young is quite different from that of the adult. Their ability to disappear into crevices in the coral suggests that their bright colouration is used not for camouflage but to advertise their territories, which they defend with vigour. In some areas the reef population works in shifts, some species occupying particular areas during the day and other species moving in at night. The Blue angelfish *Pomacanthus semicirculatus* has a series of odd markings on the tail. One particular specimen brought to the fish market in Zanzibar had the markings arranged in what appeared to be Arabic script. On one side of the tail pious Muslims read *Laillaha Illalah* (There is no God but Allah) but on the reverse side was written *Shani-Allah* (A warning sent from Allah). The fish was eventually sold for 5,000 rupees.

The mouths of butterflyfishes are small and have sharp teeth for picking small worms and other invertebrates out of cracks in the coral. In certain species, such as *Chelmon rostratus,* the snout is elongated and tube-like with the small mouth at the end, enabling the fish to poke even deeper into crevices. FAMILY: Chaetodontidae, ORDER: Perciformes, CLASS: Pisces.

BUTTONQUAILS, a family of small, skulking birds, very like quail in appearence but more closely related to the rails and cranes.

They are terrestrial and have a generally brown plumage above, usually cryptically patterned and variegated in black, buff and white, while the underside is pale, often with a spotted pattern. In some species the female is distinguished by a bright chestnut breast patch. The bill is more slender and longer than that of a quail, but some Australian species have evolved heavy, blunt bills for seed-crushing. The eyes usually have pale irises and are staring. The feet are small, with no hind-toes; the wings are rounded, and the short tail mostly concealed by the wing coverts. Buttonquails are about 4–8 in (10–20 cm) in length.

Buttonquails occur in grassland or low cover, both dry and swampy, and open woodland with some ground cover. They keep to cover and are difficult to see. If scared into flight they tend to fly low for a short distance and drop down to land again. They are, however, capable of more sustained flight and some are migratory or nomadic. The food is seeds, parts of plants, and insects. They have various whistling calls and in the widely distributed Striped buttonquail *Turnix sylvatica,* and possibly some other species, the female has a loud booming call.

There are 14 species, 13 in the typical genus *Turnix,* six of which live in Australasia. The others occur widely over the Old World, through Africa, Asia and the Oriental region, reaching Europe in southern Spain. Most species show distinct sexual dimorphism, but it is the female that is the larger and more brightly-coloured. The role of the sexes is reversed; the female displays, fighting other females and courting the males. The male incubates the eggs and cares for the chicks. It

is suspected that the female may be polyandrous, having several clutches and entrusting them to different males.

The nest is a shallow scrape, lined with dry grasses and dead leaves, on the ground in a sheltered spot. Growing grasses may be pulled downwards to conceal the nest. The clutch is usually of four eggs, rather rounded and glossy, greyish or buff with black specks and spots. The young hatch as active downy chicks. The incubation period of 12–13 days is very short for birds of this type, and the young develop rapidly, becoming independent at about 2 weeks, and adult in about 10 weeks.

In Africa a peculiar species, the lark-quail *Ortyxelos meiffrenii,* occurs on dry sandy savannah on the southern edge of the Sahara region. It is very small and sandy-coloured, patterned with black and white, and with large patches of black and white on the wings. It is a slender bird like a tiny plover or courser and has a jerky lark-like flight. It lays a clutch of only two eggs. Its call is a soft, low whistle. FAMILY: Turnicidae, ORDER: Gruiformes, CLASS: Aves.

BUZZARDS, large, broad-winged predatory birds renowned for their soaring flight, but spending much of the day perched on rocks, trees or telegraph posts. The body length is about 20 in (50·8 cm) and the wing span 3–5 ft (91·4–152·4 cm). They live in open, wooded and mountainous habitats and feed principally on ground prey of mammals and reptiles, but also take carrion and birds. Most are dark brown and superficially resemble eagles *Aquila* spp, but buzzards are smaller, have a less massive and less fierce appearance and lack the heavy bill and large claws of the eagles. There are 25 species of true buzzards included in the genus *Buteo,* with a further 10 associated genera of buzzard-like hawks which can conveniently be termed the sub-buteonines.

The buzzards belong to the family Accipitridae and the classification of this, as of all the raptor families, presents many difficulties (reasons for this are discussed more fully under falcons). It is assumed the first raptors were scavengers, so the evolutionary sequence of the Accipitridae possibly started with a kite-like raptor, then a harrier, then the true hawks and goshawks, the buzzards, with the eagles representing the most highly evolved species of the family.

Of the associated genera included as buzzards, the least buzzard-like are the buzzard-eagles *Butastur.* These are medium sized, 12–17 in (30·5–43·2 cm), with long, rather pointed, wings and a medium length tail. The bill is weak, with the basal portion

Marine butterflyfish *Pomacanthus arcuatus,* usually black with yellow bands, but sometimes with black scales edged with white.

The head of a young Rough-legged buzzard, of northern Europe.

and cere brightly coloured. The plumage is a subdued red-brown or grey. The hunting behaviour of buzzard-eagles is more like that of harriers Circinae and they prey principally on insects, reptiles and amphibians. The four species: the Grasshopper buzzard-eagle *Butastur rufipennis*; the Rufous-winged buzzard-eagle *B. liventer*; the White-eyed buzzard-eagle *B. teesa*; and the Grey-faced buzzard-eagle *B. indicus* are found in Africa and tropical Asia. *B. indicus* nests in Japan and north Asia and is migratory.

The genus *Kaupifalco* contains one species *K. monogrammicus* the Lizard buzzard. This is a plump little bird, $11\frac{1}{2}–13\frac{1}{2}$ in (29·2–34·3 cm), that lives in the African savannahs. It feeds on grasshoppers and other insects and, although it soars a good deal, it can be mistaken for a small grey sparrowhawk *Accipiter* spp.

The remaining eight genera of the buzzard-like hawks are confined to Central and South America. Like *Butastur* and *Kaupifalco* they are evidently closely related to *Buteo*, to the extent that some of the genera e.g. *Geranoaetus* and *Parabuteo* are barely distinguishable from *Buteo*. Many, however, are specialized and all are regarded as less

The typical outline of a soaring buzzard. It uses the thermals and looks very much like an eagle, for which buzzards are sometimes mistaken.

advanced in the evolutionary sense than the cosmopolitan *Buteo*. Although evidently related to each other, no accepted evolutionary sequence of the various genera has been worked out and the order in which they are considered is rather arbitrary.

Buteogallus contains three species; the Common black hawk *B. anthracinus*; the Rufous crab or Aequinoctial hawk *B. aequinoctialis*; and the Great black hawk *B. urubitinga*. They form an unusual group which include crabs in their diet in addition to frogs, reptiles, insects and small birds. Their colouration is blackish with some rufous and white banded tails. The immature plumage differs markedly from that of the adult. They are large, the Great black hawk reaching 21 in (53 cm), have coarse long legs, extremely broad wings and short square tails. The feathers of the back of the head form a slight crest and the lores and adjoining sides of the face are often bare.

The genus *Harpyhaliaetus* is closely related to *Buteogallus* and contains the Black solitary eagle *H. solitarius* and the Crowned solitary eagle *H. coronatus* which range from Mexico to central Argentina. They are larger than the previous genus, being up to 27 in (68·6 cm) long, more robust, have heavier legs and a large eagle-like bill and better developed crest. Little is known of their habits.

Busarellus contains the single medium-sized Black-collared hawk *B. nigricollis*. It is unusually coloured for a buzzard, having a bright cinnamon body, white head, black collar and wing tips. It is also unusual in being a fish-feeder and associated with this are its long legs, very heavy feet with prickly spicules on the under-side of the toes. It has been suggested this isolated genus is more akin to the Australian kite *Hamirostra*, but this resemblance is more probably a result of specialization and there is no good reason for separating it from the remainder of the neotropical buzzards. Another single-species genus *Geranoaetus* is represented by the Grey eagle-buzzard *G. melanoleucos* of the open country of western and southern South America. This large grey, mammal-eating buzzard resembles a small eagle and is sufficiently close to *Buteo* to have been united to it by some authorities. The next genus, *Heterospizias*, is also represented by only one species, the common South American Savannah or Red-winged hawk *H. meridionalis*. A medium-sized buzzard, extensively rufous in colouration, it is an opportunist feeder and has unusually long coarse legs.

The genus *Leucopternis* has ten species and is thus the largest of the sub-buteonine genera. Most are rather sluggish forest-dwellers with a slow flapping flight. They are similar to the Black hawks *Buteogallus*, but their wings are shorter and narrower. The plumage varies from nearly pure white or slate grey to striking combinations of black and white. The sides of the head are sometimes bare of feathers and then are brightly coloured like the legs. The immature birds only differ slightly from the adults. They nest in dense forests and hunt over the savannah and waterholes for reptiles, small mammals and birds. The smallest, the Black-faced hawk *L. melanops,* the White-browed hawk *L. kuhli* and the White-necked hawk *L. lacernulata,* are about 14 in (35 cm) in length. The remainder vary from 17–20 in (43–50 cm) and include the Slate-coloured hawk *L. schistacea,* the Plumbeous hawk *L. plumbea,* the Prince's hawk *L. princeps,* the Semiplumbeous hawk *L. semiplumbea,* the White hawk *L. albicollis,* the Grey-backed hawk *L. occidentalis* and the Mantled hawk *L. polionata.*

The last of the associated genera is *Parabuteo* with a single species the Bay-winged or Harris's hawk *P. unicinctus,* found from the southern United States to Chile. It is close to *Buteo,* but probably closer to *Heterospizias* and *Buteogallus.* About 20 in (51 cm) in length, rather heavy set, it has exceptionally long claws and toes, reflecting its habit of feeding on small birds. Its flight has been described as harrier-like and it possesses a white rump like the harriers.

The true buzzards (*Buteo*) possibly had their origins in South America, where so many of the sub-buteonine genera are found. They are now almost world-wide in their distribution, being absent only from Australia and most of the Indian region. Their habitat includes heavily wooded regions, mountainous areas, as well as plains, savannahs, steppes and even deserts with little tree growth. The bills and legs are medium sized, the toes short and stout. A broad wing, with from three to five of the outer primaries deeply notched, enables them to soar for very long periods; the tail is short and fan-shaped. Unlike many raptors the sexes are similar in size and colour, although there is considerable individual plumage variation and many species have colour phases. These can vary from almost black to very light individuals.

Of the 25 species, the most widely distributed is the nominate race, the Common buzzard *Buteo buteo,* originally described by Linnaeus in 1758. It breeds throughout the Palearctic region and several races have been described. Where suitable habitat exists it is found from sea level to 10,000 ft (3,000 m) and in the more northerly parts of its range it is migratory. Practically all its prey is taken on the ground, either by dropping onto it from a perch, or by diving onto it after circling or hovering briefly.

Breeding begins about February with striking aerial displays. These usually involve one or both birds circling together, interspersed with spectacular dives followed by upward swoops. The loud clear mewing note 'peee-oo' is repeatedly uttered during the display. The nest is built by both birds of the pair in a tree or on a ledge, the clutch of from two to six oval eggs being laid in late March

Buzzard with dead rabbit. When myxomatosis killed off the rabbit in western Europe, in the 1950's, the buzzard was deprived of its main prey.

or early April. They are a dull white, sparingly marked with red or brown. Incubation begins between the first and second egg and repeat clutches are rarely laid. Both sexes take part in the five-weeks incubation and the young are in the nest for 40–50 days. In the early stages the female remains at the nest with the young, while the male brings the food. After one or two weeks the female joins the male to help with the hunting. Breeding success appears to be related to food supply and varies from 1 to 3 per pair.

The Common buzzard is replaced in the north by the Rough-legged buzzard *B. lagopus*. This Holarctic species breeds between latitudes 76°N and 61°N in Europe and America. It is highly migratory, moving south in winter to southern Europe, Asia Minor and the central United States. It is rather larger and much paler than *B. buteo* and, as its name implies, has a feathered tarsus.

In the New World the niche of *B. buteo* is filled by the Red-tailed hawk *B. jamaicensis*, of eastern North America and Swainson's hawk *B. swainsonii*, of western North America. The migrations of Swainson's hawk are the most spectacular of any North American hawk, immense flocks passing each season along certain favoured routes. Other North American species include the Long-legged buzzard *B. rufinus*, the Upland buzzard *B. hemilasius*, the Ferruginous hawk *B. regalis*, the Red-shouldered hawk *B. lineatus* and the Broad-winged hawk *B. platypterus*.

The Hawaiian hawk *B. solitarius* is restricted to the Island of Hawaii, Ridgway's hawk *B. ridgwayi* is restricted to some of the Caribbean Islands and the Galapagos hawk *B. galapagoensis* is only found on the Galapagos islands. Apart from these, the remaining 13 species are mainly South American in distribution and include: the

By-the-wind sailor, an unusual jellyfish, of the kind known as siphonophores. Although typically oceanic, it is sometimes cast up on beaches in large numbers.

Red-tailed hawk *B. ventralis*, the Zone-tailed hawk *B. albonotatus*, the White-tailed hawk *B. albicaudatus*, the Jackal or Augur buzzard *B. rufofuscus*, the African Mountain buzzard *B. oreophilus*, the Madagascar buzzard *B. brachypterus*, the African Red-tailed buzzard *B. auguralis*, the Short-tailed hawk *B. brachyurus*, the Rufous-thighed hawk *B. leucorrhous*, the Red-backed buzzard *B. polyosoma*, Gurney's buzzard *B. poecilochrous*, the Roadside, Insect, Large-billed or Tropical broad-winged hawk *B. magnirostris*, and the Grey hawk, Mexican goshawk or Shining buzzard-hawk *B. nitidus*. The last two are somewhat more primitive than the remainder of the *Buteo* and probably form a link between them and the sub-buteonine genera. FAMILY: Accipitridae, ORDER: Falconiformes, CLASS: Aves.
I.P.

BY-THE-WIND SAILOR *Velella*, a kind of jellyfish, known as a siphonophore, living in the warmer oceans and the Mediterranean. It has a flat almost oblong float like a miniature raft, with a transparent gas-filled triangular sail on its upper surface, which the wind catches and drives the animal along the surface of the sea. The raft is deep blue and up to $2\frac{1}{2}$ in (63 mm) long and $1\frac{1}{2}$ in (38 mm) broad. On the undersurface is a central mouth surrounded by rings of reproductive bodies or gonophores and, outside these, by a ring of delicate mobile tentacles round the margin of the float. These are heavily charged with stinging cells for the capture of food and for the animal's protection. The gonophores bud off small male and female medusae which lack a mouth. After release from the gonophores they produce eggs and sperm. They were named *Chrysomitra*, since they were originally thought to represent a separate genus. ORDER: Athecata, CLASS: Hydrozoa, PHYLUM: Cnidaria.

CACIQUE, the common name for tropical birds of the genus *Cacicus* (11 species) of the family of the New World orioles, which are confined to tropical Central and South America. The best known are the Yellow-rumped cacique *Cacicus cela,* which is black with yellow on the wings and a yellow rump and the Red-rumped cacique *Cacicus haemorrhous,* which is bluish black with a red rump. They live and nest in a colony, sometimes both species in mixed colonies which consist of a cluster of basket-like nests with the entrance right at the top and often around a wasp nest in trees and shrubbery. Nest building, incubation and feeding of the nestlings is done by the female only. Caciques feed on fruits and insects. FAMILY: Icteridae, ORDER: Passeriformes, CLASS: Aves.

CACOMISTLE, or Ring-tailed 'cat', closely related to the raccoon, this small carnivore might be mistaken for a 'mini' raccoon, but has a more slender build and the black and white ringed tail is longer than the body. It does not have a black mask either. Instead, two pinkish buff patches are present above and below the eyes. The long, soft fur on the back is grey with black-tipped guard hairs contrasting with the creamy white underside. Cat-sized, cacomistles measure 24·2–32 in (61–81 cm), the tail being slightly longer than the head and body. Weights vary from 1·8–2·2 lb (0·85–1 kg).

They are found in the western USA south to Central America and two species exist. The cacomistle *Bassariscus astutus* has small paws with semi-retractile claws and haired soles and large round ears which are thinly furred. The rarer Mexican cacomistle *Bassariscus sumichrasti,* which lives in the forested areas of Central America is more arboreal than its northern counterpart. This species has pointed ears, naked soles, non-retractile claws and a longer tail to further differentiate it.

These animals are nocturnal and have the same arboreal agility and rapidity as some

Cacomistle or Ring-tailed 'cat', capable of leaps of 3 m from one rocky ledge to another.

mustelids, such as martens. Found in desert mountain areas or in forests, cacomistles often remain close to human habitations to hunt rodents, insects and birds and to eat fruit. Trappers and gold miners frequently kept these attractive animals as pets, hence the popular name Ring-tailed 'cat', indicative of their tameness and mousing capacities. The northern species mates in April and three to four young are born in May or June. The Mexican cacomistle, on the other hand, breeds in January and the cubs are born in March. Weighing slightly over 1 oz (30 gm) at birth, the young are blind and lightly furred. Only the female visits the grass-lined nest hidden under a rock or in a hollow tree trunk for the first three weeks. The ringed tail and grey fur appear when the young are a month old. Although they are not fully weaned until four months, the eight-week-old cubs leave the nest to follow their parents on hunting forays. When suddenly taken off guard, cacomistles emit a spluttering bark and briefly erect the fur of the tail. During the breeding season, the male and female, which are solitary during most of the year, call to each other with a long, modulated mewing sound. The 'contact' call between mother and young is a short series of low chirps. Native hunters claim that a cacomistle's lair is always found near water and that, when located in a tree, it can easily be identified as the bark around the entrance hole has invariably been chewed away. Whether this is entirely true is not certain, but cacomistles sometimes take over squirrels' empty nests which might well have gnawed the bark for food. FAMILY: Procyonidae, ORDER: Carnivora, CLASS: Mammalia.   N.D.

CADDIS FLIES, a group of moth-like flies closely related to the moths and butterflies, from which they may be distinguished by the possession, to a greater or lesser extent, of hairs instead of scales on the wings. Trichoptera, the order to which Caddis flies belong, literally means 'hairy-winged'. The wings of Caddis flies are held tentwise over the body and are never held vertically upwards as are those of butterflies and, as in moths, mandibles are absent. The antennae are slender, thread-like and sometimes exceptionally long, as in the family Leptoceridae, where they are as much as three times the length of the body. In contrast with the Lepidoptera (moths and butterflies), however, Caddis flies are most often drably coloured, browns and yellows predominating, while a number are blackish. Some are green or white, a few show iridescence and one is bright blue. They are mostly small to moderate in size and although very few can be considered large, many species, especially those in the family Hydroptilidae, are extremely small. These latter are also very agile and often to be found running over the

surfaces of stones or rocks adjacent to water and may only, with difficulty, be distinguished from small moths.

They are found throughout the world and about 3,000 species are known in 18 families. They have not been widely studied in the past, but now numbers of new species are being described from various parts of the world. With only very few exceptions, the immature stages of Caddis flies are aquatic so that the adult flies are to be found in the vicinity of water, although many species, being attracted to light, sometimes wander a few miles. Almost every situation where fresh, unpolluted water flows or collects will be found to contain a caddis fauna, even on the surface of wet rocks, deep in caves and boggy seepages on mountain tops, but they are not so evident by large lakes in tropical areas. Apparently in such locations it is only where there is wave action near the shore that conditions are suitable for the development of the larvae. In some parts of the world they exist in such large numbers that they assume pest proportions, causing jamming of air-conditioning plants and making outdoor activities impossible at the periods of maximum emergence.

With the exception of the very few terrestrial species, the eggs of Caddis flies are laid either above the water or actually in it. If

the former is the case the larvae hatch out of a jelly-like egg-mass during rain and find their way into the water. Members of the family Hydropsychidae, on the other hand, have been seen to enter the water and lay their eggs under stones in fast-flowing water.

The females of some species carry the partially extruded egg-mass about for some time before depositing it. One such species, *Brachycentrus subnubilus,* is known as the greentail for this reason. In many cases the egg-mass has no distinctive shape but in the family Phryganeidae it is in the form of a ring which hangs on aquatic plants or adheres to their surfaces. It is soft and gelatinous in texture and the eggs may be seen clearly within it, arranged in transverse discs. In the genus *Triaenodes* the eggs are laid in a disc and arranged spirally.

The larval stage of Caddis flies is almost certainly better known than the adults as the larvae of many species construct a case for themselves which is of such a size that when the larva is feeding or pulling itself along by its rather spidery legs, the abdomen is contained within it and, indeed, held fast to it by a pair of hooked appendages situated at the hind end. When alarmed or resting the larva can retract itself completely within its case. So that respiration can take place there are various devices to enable water to flow

The larva of the Caddis fly *Hydropsyche* (top) showing tufts of gills on thorax and abdomen. The centre drawing shows the adult Caddis fly *Phryganea obsoleta*. The bottom drawing shows a larva of *Limnophilus centralis* emerging from its case of tiny Water snail shells.

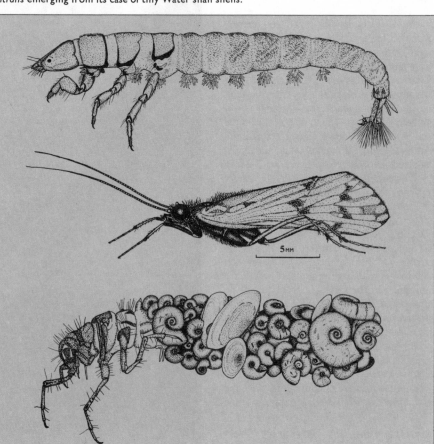

Adult Caddis fly *Stenophylax permistus*, typically drab coloured, always found near water in which eggs are laid and the larvae live.

continuously through the case. In most of the case-bearing caddis larvae, three finger-like projections occur on the first segment of the abdomen, one at the top and one on each side. This neatly spaces out the front end of the body and, indeed, helps to grip the case, at the same time allowing the free flow of water backwards. In most of the species the abdomen, covered with a number of filament-like gills, is in a state of continuous movement and with a pump-like motion draws the water through the case. An additional device found in the larvae of a large number of species is a sieve which, whilst allowing the water to leave the case after aerating the gill-filaments, does not allow the entry of predacious insects.

The larval case is made of a wide variety of materials which can be collected by the caddis larva in the water and comes in a wide range of patterns. The pattern for each species is constant, although, according to availability, there may be some variation in the material used for construction. In order to cement the pieces together, a silk-like secretion is produced from the mouth and in a number of species the whole case is made of this substance which takes on a leathery or horny consistency. In the family Phryganeidae the case is commonly made from a

number of small rectangular pieces cut from leaves, or sometimes pieces of stalk, and arranged in a spiral fashion. This pattern is also adopted by a few species in the family Leptoceridae and the common European species, *Triaenodes bicolor,* is an example not only of the spiral case, but also of a swimming caddis, the larva propelling itself in its case by oar-like movements of its long, fringed pair of hindlegs. In the family Limnephilidae the case is usually tubular.

A number of unusual objects are often used in case construction. For example *Limnephilus flavicornis* will utilize small Water snails for its case whenever they are available. Often a caddis case is very delicately constructed, especially those made of small pebbles or sand grains, so the case becomes virtually invisible on the sandy bed of a stream or river.

Although most cases are circular or oval in transverse section there are a number of instances of other geometrical patterns. In *Lepidostoma hirtum* in the Sericostomatidae, the case is made of plates of vegetable debris placed so as to provide a square section and in *Crunoecia irrorata,* in the same family, the back end is circular and the front end is rectangular in section. A number of caddis cases are made of circular pieces cut from

submerged leaves making a flat case, but the African species, *Leptocerina ramosa pinheyi,* makes its case of three elongated pieces cut from aquatic grasses and this gives a triangular transverse section. *Anabolia nervosa* adopts an unusual procedure in fastening one or two fairly large twigs, sometimes 3 in ($7\frac{1}{2}$ cm) or so in length, to its sand-grain case. It is thought that this might make it difficult for a trout, for instance, having taken the case into its mouth to blow the larva out as it is able to do with other simpler cases.

In a number of families the larva constructs a case only when it is about to pupate. Thus, for example, in the genus *Rhyacophila* the larva is free-living and wanders over moss-covered stones in search of its prey which consists of smaller aquatic creatures. Many larvae spin nets of a silk-like material in the form of small sheets or bags which are usually placed where the water currents are most rapid. The larvae often have mouthparts adapted not only to seize and eat small aquatic animals, but also to brush diatoms and small algal filaments off the net and consume them.

In the family Psychomyiidae the larvae construct a silken tunnel several times their own length, fastened to a rock or submerged branch. They then station themselves at the tunnel entrance and presumably seize small organisms as they are carried along by the current.

A cocoon is formed in preparation for the change to the pupal stage. The case-bearing larvae usually plug the ends of the larval case, while the net-spinners, the tunnel-makers and the free-living species construct a new, usually dome-shaped, case of rock fragments, small pebbles, sand grains or vegetable debris.

The pupal caddis is very like the adult fly but covered with a thin cuticle and having three rather extraordinary mechanisms. Strong mandibles are present by means of which a way is cut out of the enveloping cocoon; a pair of processes at the end of the abdomen enable sieves of the cocoon to be cleaned when the abdomen is twisted around; and pairs of hook plates on the abdominal segments allow the pupa to work its way out of the cocoon and then to swim by means of its heavily hair-fringed legs to the water surface. On arrival at the surface the active pupa either crawls out onto a stone or up a plant stem, or floats on the water surface, bursts the pupal skin and the adult crawls out after untwining the long antennae from its complex folds.

Caddis larvae, by virtue of their large numbers, and in many cases large size, play an important role in freshwater environments by cutting up vegetable material, living or dead, for case construction and for food. In addition, they remove diatoms and algal felt from the substrate and feed on a wide range of freshwater animals, including species in their own order. On the other hand, larval, pupal and adult caddis form a not inconsiderable part of the diet of freshwater fishes, and in some cases, of birds and bats as well. ORDER: Trichoptera, CLASS: Insecta, PHYLUM: Arthropoda.   N.E.H.

CAECILIANS, long-bodied, limbless amphibians without common names which superficially resemble large earthworms. They are invariably blind and the eyes are covered with opaque skin, or in some cases by the bones of the skull. There is a small sensory tentacle just in front of each eye, lying in a sac from which it can be protruded. The tentacle has two ducts which communicate with Jacobson's organ, a sensory area adjacent to the nasal cavity. There is no tympanic membrane and it is likely that caecilians 'hear' by picking up vibrations in the ground via their lower jaw. Caecilians move, like snakes, by sinuous lateral undulations of the body. Many are able to burrow quite rapidly and the majority spend most of their time below ground level. A number of species are, however, aquatic. Caecilians vary considerably in size. The largest *Caecilia thompsoni,* from Central Colombia, reaches a length of

55 in (139·7 cm), the smallest is *Hypogeophis brevis,* from the Seychelles in the Indian Ocean, 4½ in (11·2 cm) long. The maximum diameter recorded for any caecilian is 1 in (2·5 cm). A picture is shown on page 61.

The body of caecilians is divided by a number of folds in the skin which give a ringed appearance, as in an earthworm. Many species bear small scales in pockets just below the epidermis. The scales are small, rounded and composed of a large number of plates. The presence of scales in the caecilians is considered to be a primitive character since the ancestors of the modern amphibians had scales although all other living amphibians are scaleless.

In the majority of caecilians the hind end is short and rounded, but a few species have a small 'tail'. The vent may be a longitudinal, circular or transverse opening. Externally the sexes cannot be separated but the male has an intromittent organ, a modified portion of the gut which can be everted. Fertilization is therefore internal. Some species, such as *Ichthyophis,* lay eggs in cavities in the mud or among rocks close to water. The female usually coils around the developing eggs. The larvae develop within the egg capsule and although gills are present these are resorbed before hatching. Others lay eggs which develop into free-swimming larvae with external gills. In other species the eggs are retained and develop within the mother, some species producing live young which have developed outside the egg-capsule within the mother.

The left lung in caecilians is very small, the right one is large and long. Respiration is probably also through the skin which is well supplied with dermal glands that keep it moist. The skull, which is very hard and compact, consists of a few large bones, its structure related to the burrowing habit. The lower jaw has a large jaw muscle, and the jaw is opened by raising the skull rather than by dropping the lower jaw. Ribs are present but there is no trace of limbs or limb girdles.

Little is known of the biology of caecilians since they are often difficult to find and have only infrequently been kept in captivity. They are apparently carnivorous and feed on earthworms and small insects, especially termites. They need moist surroundings and are usually drab in colour although some have a little colour. *Rhinatrema,* for example, may have a vivid yellow strip along the side of the body.

The 158 species of caecilians are distributed throughout the warm-temperate regions of the Old and the New World from sea level to around 6,000 ft (2,000 m). They are virtually unknown as fossils. ORDER: Apoda (or Gymnophiona), CLASS: Amphibia.
                                                          R.L.

CAGE BIRDS, birds kept in captivity for study, show or aesthetic enjoyment. Millions

of birds, of many species, are kept in ordinary homes for the pleasure of having a bird as a pet. In addition, 'bird fanciers' keep and breed birds which must conform to certain set show standards established by 'the fancy'. Also, aviculturists keep birds for study and the simple pleasure of keeping them, and large numbers of birds are kept in cages in scientific establishments for observational and experimental purposes. A considerable number of people derive their income from supplying these different birds, their food and their equipment.

The keeping of birds in cages is probably older than the true domestication of birds because primitive peoples seem to have a natural interest in birds as part of their environment. The children of certain tribes of today, Eskimos for example, not uncommonly keep stray or orphan birds and other animals, and it is probable that they have long done so. It is also likely that in prehistoric times birds were kept in confinement for future eating when captured in excess numbers. Such activities could have contributed to the development of the keeping of birds in captivity for pleasure in a more aesthetic sense.

Whatever the origins of bird-keeping, birds have been domesticated from the time of the first written records, around 3,000 BC, in Egypt where pigeons were used for food and for carrying messages. Geese, ducks and the domestic hen were established in captivity shortly afterwards in various parts of the world and by the time the Romans reached Britain domestic fowl were kept for cock-fighting as well as for food.

The current interest in cage and aviary birds has had a long historical development, with bird catchers plying their trade for many centuries, but the real impetus came when the ornithologist, John Gould, first successfully introduced the budgerigar *Melopsittacus undulatus* from Australia in 1840. There may now be 5 million of these birds in Britain alone, far surpassing the total of any other species. Like the wild form today the budgerigars first brought to Europe were, as Gould put it, 'pre-eminent both for beauty of plumage and elegance of form'. Selective breeding of different types, with consequent exaggeration of certain features such as the head, and reduction of general fitness, has rather changed the bird, but it is still a creature of great charm and popularity.

The wild-type budgerigar, which is in fact a small parakeet, is bright green on the back and underparts, with mantle and wings finely barred with greenish yellow and darker

Zebra finch, said to be the commonest of all cage birds. From the wild bird have been bred three colour varieties: fawn, silver and white.

markings. The tail is dark green-blue in the centre, patterned with blue and yellow at the sides. From this form have been bred all the varieties of blue, violet, white and yellow 'budgies' which, as well as the green, are so common today.

In the 1920s and 1930s the budgerigar was less common as a cage bird than it is now, the canary *Serinus canaria* being far more popular. The latter species, found wild in the Canary Islands, Madeira and the Azores, was first imported into Europe in the 16th century. The wild bird is a typical small finch, greyish green above, yellow on the breast and rump, with darker streaks in the centre of the feathers. From this form have been bred the 'type' canaries of various shapes and sizes such as the Norwich, Border and Lizard varieties, and the 'song' canaries such as the Roller. Many colour varieties have been bred, including white, yellow, orange and fawn. Even a red canary has been developed by crossing with the Hooded siskin *Carduelis cucculatus*.

Hybrids are also obtained by crossing the canary with other species such as the green-finch *Carduelis chloris* and the goldfinch *C. carduelis*. The offspring are called mules, and the breeding of these has a definite, if restricted popularity.

The canary and other finches mentioned above are true finches belonging to the family Fringillidae. Other common cage birds, only some of which are called finches, notably the Bengalese finch, Zebra finch, and the Java sparrow, belong to the Weaver finch family, Estrildidae. The Bengalese is a form of the oriental Sharp-tailed finch *Lonchura striata*, long domesticated and bred in Japan after being introduced there from China. The domesticated birds are very tolerant of poor conditions and will live in small cages on a monotonous diet. The wild, and some domestic birds are dull chocolate brown above, whitish below. Other birds are fawn or white. The Zebra finch *Poephila castanotis* is a native of Australia and in its wild form is grey-brown above, white below, with a black, white and orange face, barred upper breast separated from the white underparts by a black band, chestnut flanks spotted with white, black and white-barred tail and red bill. The female is somewhat duller. It is about the same size as the Bengalese finch, that is rather smaller than a canary. These, however, are not the smallest of the frequently-kept cage birds being larger than a number of African waxbills and fire-finches commonly offered for sale. The Java sparrow *Padda oryzivora*, however, a native of Java and other parts of Southeast Asia, is a large striking estrildine with basically blue-grey plumage, a black rump and tail and a

Indian hill mynah, one of the best bird mimics.

black head with white cheeks and a massive pink bill. White and pied forms are also common in domestication. The sexes are very similar in appearance.

Other species more commonly thought of as songbirds are sometimes kept and bred in captivity. Other finches such as the bullfinch *Pyrrhula pyrrhula*, larks, thrushes and even warblers and nightingales are kept. In fact cage bird enthusiasts may attempt to keep and breed almost any species, from hummingbirds to birds of prey, and from woodpeckers to Birds of paradise. And collections of such birds as waterfowl and pheasants are becoming more numerous every year.

One group which has increased greatly in popularity is the parrot family, Psittacidae, the best known, apart from the budgerigar, probably being the African grey parrot *Psittacus erithacus* and the lovebirds *Agapornis* spp. One of the attractions of the parrot group is their ability to mimic human speech and other sounds. This also accounts for the

popularity of the Indian hill mynah *Gracula religiosa*, though the most outstanding mimic of all is probably the Spotted bower-bird *Chlamydera maculata* of Australia. Certain of the crows, such as the magpie *Pica pica* and the jay *Garrulus glandarius* are also kept for their ability as mimics as well as their beautiful plumage.

Another group found in large numbers, both of individuals and of species, is the Columbidae—pigeons and doves. Many varieties have been developed from the Rock dove *Columba livia*, a blue-grey bird with two black bars on the wings. The feral pigeons of towns and cities, the descendants of lost tame pigeons, exist in a number of colour forms but tend to revert to the original type. Some of the domesticated forms are rather grotesque, including the Fairy swallows with feet and legs thickly covered with large feathers, show fantails with 'pigeon' chests and heads thrown back onto their tails and carrier pigeons with large fleshy outgrowths on the bill. Other species are kept in their original form, for example the tiny Diamond dove *Geopelia cuneata* of Australia, and the Barbary dove, derived with little change from the African form of the Collared dove *Streptopelia decaocto roseogrisea*. It is an Asiatic form of this species, *Streptopelia d. decaocto*, which has spread across Europe so rapidly, now breeding over much of Britain.

Usually when people think of 'cage birds' they think of birds as pets, in 'the fancy' or in aviculture. But we must remember that as many, if not more birds are kept in cages for experimental purposes, discounting the millions of battery fowls used for food produc-

Java sparrow, popular cage bird, bred in two varieties, grey and white.

tion. In laboratories all over the world pigeons, domestic fowl and other species are kept for the study of problems such as imprinting, learning and memory. For example, much has been learnt about celestial navigation from studies with caged warblers and starlings, and experiments with canaries and crows have taught us much about avian intelligence. Cage birds can have many more uses than the detection of poisonous gases in mines—a long-established function of canaries. Attempts are even being made in the United States, and probably in other countries, to employ birds instead of humans in operative tasks which are boring or dangerous. Here, as in other aspects of bird-keeping, ethical problems may arise. P.M.D.

CAHOW. The Gadfly petrels *Pterodroma* spp, are medium-sized seabirds nesting on oceanic islands. The birds and their eggs were much sought after by early human settlers for food, and introduced animals later killed many more birds, so that several species are now near extinction. The cahow *P. cahow* of Bermuda was thought to have been exterminated about 1621 but was rediscovered at the beginning of this century. In 1951 a small nesting colony was found and by protection this has increased to perhaps 80 birds. The species is now threatened by DDT residues which have brought about a decline in nesting success. FAMILY: Procellariidae, ORDER: Procellariiformes, CLASS: Aves.

CAIMAN LIZARD *Dracaena guianensis*, 3–4 ft (90–120 cm) long, lives along both brackish and freshwater shorelines of Brazilian and Guiana waterways. Superficially it resembles the caiman of that area, its enlarged dorsal scales looking like the raised osteoderms on crocodilians. It feeds mainly on molluscs, crushing these between its powerful jaws armed with large, oval crushing rear teeth, the mollusc being held in place by the tongue and muscular gum-folds that enclose the teeth.

Although these lizards may locate and retrieve their prey underwater, unlike the crocodilians they devour their food on shore (in captivity, at least). FAMILY: Teiidae, ORDER: Squamata, CLASS: Reptilia.

CAIMANS, tropical cousins of the alligator, in the 100 million year old crocodilian order. Except in scientific publications the caiman is usually erroneously called an alligator. Few people would buy a caiman skin handbag, so hide dealers simply use the skin of the caiman and the name of the more widely known alligator. Live baby South American Spectacled caimans, *Caiman crocodylus crocodylus*, imported into the United States for the pet trade, are sold as alligators also.

Cockatiel, or cockatoo-parrot, a decorative longtailed parrot popular with bird-fanciers.

Caimans as a group are smaller in size than the other crocodilians but possess the same general characteristics. The caiman's powerful tail, lashing from side to side, propels him through water at a rapid rate. The back has a tough hide reinforced by bony plates. The throat contains a fleshy flap that can be closed to permit breathing at the water's surface with only the tip of the nose showing. The nostrils have external valves and the eyes are doubly protected by eye lids and a movable, clear membrane. The teeth of the lower jaw fit into pits in the upper jaw when the jaws are closed.

The Smooth-fronted caiman, *Paleosuchus trigonatus*, and the Dwarf caiman *Paleosuchus palpebrosus*, from the Amazon, are the smallest of the caimans. To protect their bodies from rapids in the swift waters they inhabit, the bony plates in the armour of these small creatures extend down to the belly. As an adaptation for survival against modern man's destruction the armour of these caimans is more effective than the awesome jaws of a crocodile because it renders the skin useless for the world's hide industries.

Caimans occur only in the western hemisphere. South America contains most of the eight species of caiman. The huge Black caiman *Melanosuchus niger* reaches a length of 15 ft (4·6 m) in the Amazon basin and Guiana region. Central America is the home of the Dusky caiman, *Caiman crocodylus fuscus*.

The Spectacled caiman from the Amazon and Orinoco regions has been introduced into the swamps of the southern United States and has survived. Most people, after they have brought their exotic baby caiman, decide the animal is more than they can handle, and release it. Evidently the caiman colonies in the United States represent these released babies.

The potential life span of the caiman can approach 40 years. Most caimans reach sexual maturity at a length of 5 or 6 ft (1·5–1·8 m). It is rare if one caiman reaches adult size from an average hatch of two

Black caiman, one of the eight species of crocodilian peculiar to South America.

dozen young. There are many predators that eat caiman eggs. Turtles, rodents, crocodilians and birds take a heavy toll of eggs and young.

Mating occurs with the male mounting the female in the water and twisting his tail beneath hers to accomplish a union. Approximately one month after conception the female builds a nest close to a stream, composed of decaying leaves and branches. The nest is shaped into a mound by the female using her feet to throw the rotting debris while gradually backing around the nest. The eggs are laid only a few inches deep in the mound. The female repairs any damage to the nest and keeps the rotting vegetation and eggs damp by constantly crawling from the water to the top of the mound. The heat from the decaying vegetation keeps the eggs at a constant 90°F (32°C). Observations made on the breeding habits of captive Spectacled caimans at the Atlanta Zoological Park, USA, indicate that the female protects the nest from small predators such as turtles, but not from man. If the female guarding the nest is killed the eggs will not survive in the wild.

When the young in the eggs are ready to hatch they respond to any activity on the mound by making 'croaking' sounds. The female caiman hears the young and digs down to them. The young usually hatch the moment the rotting vegetation is removed and rush for the nearest water.

Young caimans grow rapidly and eat huge quantities of crayfish, fish, insects, snails, snakes and small rodents. Within three years the 8 in (20 cm) hatchlings reach a length of 3 ft (90 cm). The same growth rate can be obtained in captivity if the caimans are kept

at a temperature of 85°F (29°C) and fed a varied diet. Larger caimans occasionally catch land animals that come to the water to drink but they never prey on man.

Caimans and many other crocodilians are doomed to extinction because of man's quest for their skins. It would be one of the greatest tragedies in the earth's evolutionary history if an animal that has survived for millions of years was exterminated for a few handbags and shoes. FAMILY: Alligatoridae, ORDER: Crocodilia, CLASS: Reptilia.   H.H.

CAKE URCHIN, see Sand dollar.

CALANUS, a tiny marine crustacean common in most seas and the dominant copepod of the northern North Sea and the waters to the north and west of the British Isles. Here two slightly different forms occur, *C. finmarchicus* and *C. helgolandicus*; the latter more commonly found in the southern parts of the area.

Most copepods are no bigger than a pinhead but *Calanus* is about the size of a grain of rice. It belongs to the Gymnoplea a group in which all the limbs are on the long oval-shaped front part of the body, leaving the short narrow tail-piece limbless. *Calanus* is beautifully transparent except for spots of scarlet pigment which may at times colour the whole body. Conspicuous at the front of the animal are the first antennae, a pair of segmented feelers which are slightly longer than the body and in the living animal are usually at right angles to the body. On the underside of the main body, which is divided into a head and segmented thoracic region, there are six pairs of thoracic limbs of which the first are modified for feeding. The remainder are typical biramous crustacean limbs, except that they are flattened like paddles for swimming.

Reproduction is sexual. Sperms are produced in an elongated spermatophore. During mating, the spermatophore is transferred by the male to the genital segment of the female. The eggs are fertilized probably at the moment of extrusion. On average a female lays 2–300 eggs in a series of bursts, each lasting about a week. They are shed into the water where they adhere in somewhat pear-shaped clumps. The number of eggs laid depends very much on how much food has been eaten by the female. Some females,

The copepod *Calanus helgolandicus*, a major food of herring and many other fishes and invertebrates.

although ready to lay eggs, do not necessarily do so at once and it has been suggested that they may be able to delay egg-laying until conditions are favourable, which could explain why egg-laying in *Calanus* often seems to coincide with increases in numbers of diatoms. Eggs seem to be laid mostly at night and from the time of extrusion they take about 20 hours to hatch at 68°F (20°C) and 60 hours at 41°F (5°C).

After hatching, *Calanus* passes through a series of larval stages, six naupliar and five copepodite stages. Between each stage, the animal sheds its outer skin of rigid chitin and increases in size before the new skin hardens. Life-span from egg to mature adult varies considerably with season and latitude, being longest in the far north where it is a little over a year. Growth rate in the different larval stages is not uniform but tends to slow down in the more advanced instars. Egg-laying takes place mostly from early spring to summer and after July many individuals remain in the last copepodite stage and, especially in the Arctic, these individuals overwinter in deep water.

One of the outstanding activities of *Calanus* is a well-marked vertical migration, which varies with season and in some seasons with alternation of day and night. In winter, *Calanus* generally remains in deep water and does not migrate, but from January onwards an ascent begins and breeding takes place in the surface layers. When the water is warm, on certain sunny days in May and June, it is not uncommon to see in places, such as the River Clyde, the surface of the sea covered with small expanding ripples as though it

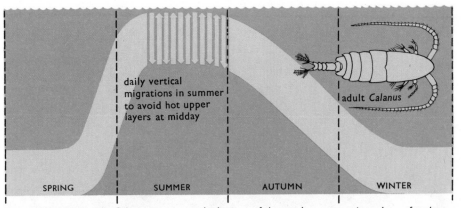

daily vertical migrations in summer to avoid hot upper layers at midday

adult *Calanus*

SPRING SUMMER AUTUMN WINTER

During the cold months *Calanus* remains at the bottom of the sea. It moves up into the surface layers in summer but there makes a daily vertical migration swimming downwards each morning to avoid the warmer water heated by the sun.

were raining. These spots are often caused by congregations of enormous numbers of *Calanus*. Frequently, in summer, *Calanus* migrates downwards by day and returns to the surface by night. This behaviour is often called diurnal migration and is seemingly a response primarily to light, though perhaps modified by temperature. It has been suggested that the animal is attempting to adapt itself to an optimum light intensity. The extent of this vertical migration varies greatly from place to place, from season to season, between different instars and even from day to day.

Calanus is widespread in all oceans except the Antarctic. In northern seas, it is outstanding as one of the main links between the floating plants of the sea and fishes. It forms, for instance, a staple part of the food of the herring, which is in turn one of the most

abundant of the fishes caught in the seas off northwest Europe. ORDER: Calanoida, CLASS: Crustacea, SUB-CLASS: Copepoda, PHYLUM: Arthropoda. W.J.P.S.

CAMEL. There are two species of camel both belonging to the Old World: the One-humped or Arabian camel *Camelus dromedarius,* of North Africa and the Near East, and the Two-humped or Bactrian camel *C. bactrianus,* of Asia. The first is not known in the wild, the second survives in the wild in the Gobi Desert. The One-humped camel is commonly referred to as the dromedary, a name which strictly speaking should be reserved for a special breed used in riding.

Camels are up to 9 ft (3 m) long and stand nearly 7 ft (2·2 m) at the shoulder. The legs are long, the neck is long and curved, the ears are small, the eyes have long lashes and the nostrils can be closed as an additional protection against blown sand. The foot consists of two toes united at the sole by a web of skin. There are horny callosities on the chest and leg joints. The dental formula is: $i \frac{1}{3} c \frac{1}{1} pm \frac{3}{2} m \frac{3}{3}$.

Because of its fleshy lips and long papillae on the inside of the mouth a camel can eat hard thorny food. It will eat almost any kind of dry vegetation and while food is abundant fat accumulates in the hump as an energy store.

When Arabian and Bactrian camels live side by side as in Asia Minor, southern Russia and Syria they frequently cross-breed, the offspring being known as tulus which are valued for their strength and because their usefulness as domestic animals is not marred by breeding periods.

The Arabian camel is more slender, with a shorter coat than the Bactrian and the colour of the coat is more variable. There are many skewbalds but the white dromedaries are valued most. The Arabic vocabulary comprises 1,000 expressions referring to camels alone. The Arabian camel was probably first domesticated by nomadic tribes from the interior of Arabia. However, it was first

The female of the copepod *Calanus helgolandicus* shown on the left, but this time in side view. The underwater photograph clearly shows the antennae folded back to give least resistance to the water as the thoracic legs drive the animal forwards.

mentioned as a domestic animal in the 11th century BC in Palestine at the time of the Midianite invasions. In the 9th century BC it was used in the Assyrian campaigns against the Arabs in Mesopotamia and has been used in Egypt since the 3rd century. It is generally assumed that it reached the rest of North Africa in the first centuries AD. Many authors believe, however, by reason of rock paintings and bone discoveries, that it was already known as a domestic animal in northwest Africa in the Stone Age and has not left that area since.

The Arabian camel is found throughout the whole of the Sahara from Mauretania to Somaliland, across Arabia to Syria, Iran, Afghanistan and northern India, its southern limit of distribution in Africa being the latitude 13°N. Northwards it is spread beyond the Caspian Sea to Russian Turkestan where, as in Asia Minor, Arabian camels appear together with the Two-humped camel. They were introduced later to southwest Africa and Australia where they are to be encountered at the present time in large, feral herds.

Caravans cover only about 20–25 miles (30–40 km) a day, but the camel is superior to the horse in its steady trot, which if necessary it can keep up all day. Record performances of 125 miles (200 km) a day have been known, but the animals only recovered from these after months of rest. In the cool season camels can travel across 620 miles (1,000 km) of waterless desert. They have a strong homing instinct and often escape from distant areas to their original home 300 miles (500 km) or even 620 miles (1,000 km) away.

In the Sahara the formation of herds is usually controlled by human beings. In summer most of the herds are unattended and then often form themselves into mixed herds, bands of stallions, groups of mares and their

Male Arabian camels get to grips after a bout of threatening.   Camels facing sun, exposing minimum body surface to the heat.

Well-laden Ship of the Desert.

These camels are drinking at a well near Darawar in West Pakistan.

young; many, particularly older animals, also go solitary. In the mating season, from January to April the stallion will tolerate no rivals and the herds must always be watched. Their owners separate them into three different kinds: those with a leader stallion and up to 30 mares and their yearlings and two-year-olds; herds of geldings, young and entire stallions; and herds of mares and their new-born foals.

Stallions have a remarkable threatening behaviour: if two leader stallions meet, they threaten each other while already far off. They stretch out their necks, gnash their teeth, spit and lash the tail up and down. When they get nearer they emit a 'blo-blo-blo' sound, lowering the head, then raising it above the horizontal and at the same time protruding a red pouch from the side of the mouth which seems to be absent in the Two-humped camel stallion. The throat pouch is also projected in front of the mare not only during mating but also often out of the breeding season. Geldings only rarely project this pouch and usually not completely.

Gestation is 12–13 months and lactation lasts 1–2 years. The mares foal every second year and go apart from the herd, to give birth

Dromedary, breed of Arabian camel for riding.

Baby camel being suckled.

Camel caravan in the Negev Desert.

either lying or standing. The foal can run after 2–3 hours, first of all in a mixture of stagger and amble, and not later than the second day it can amble confidently.

The astonishing performances of the camel, outstandingly adapted as it is to life in the desert, have since time immemorial given rise to many legends, which even today have not been entirely erased from popular beliefs. The most famous is the legend about storing water in the stomach. In 1954/55 the physiologists K. and B. Schmidt-Nielsen investigated the camel's capacity for water storage. They proved that the 'water cells' in the paunch, which Pliny long ago regarded as water reservoirs, cannot hold more than 11 pints (5 litres) and usually they contain only a wet chyme. In no case was stored drinking water found. The hump is equally unimportant in the water economy. Thus, the consumption of fat yields exactly as much water as the weight of the fat, but this process of combustion requires oxygen, which involves additional work for the lungs and thus a loss of water through exhalation. In the end exactly the same amount of water is lost as is formed from the fat. The hump, which at best weighs 88 lb (40 kg) is an energy store.

A camel does not drink for the future, but for the past. It drinks only as much water as it has lost since the last watering through sweat, urine and faeces. This loss is unusually small, chiefly due to the high variability of the body temperature. Whereas other mammals and human beings prevent overheating of the body by perspiration, the thirsty camel can raise its temperature by 9°F (6°C) without getting feverish. As the air temperature rises, the body temperature gradually rises from 91°F (34°C) to almost 106°F (41°C) and it is then only that the excess heat is eliminated by perspiration. In winter and when the animal is not thirsty the daily fluctuations of the body temperature amount to only 3·5°F (2°C).

The thick coat also gives protection from loss of heat, as also does the camels' habit of lying close together in small groups, just when the heat is greatest. This reduces the areas of the body exposed to the sun and undoubtedly one animal receives from its fellows less heat than it would were it directly exposed to the sun. Then the coat can heat up to 177°F (80°C). Moreover, when the heat is great, camels always lie facing the sun. This surprising behaviour is also an effective protection from heat. The animals remain in the same place all day long, merely adjusting their position to that of the sun. To change places frequently would entail greater heating, since the ground becomes very hot as the day wears on.

Arab police patrol, Wadi Rum, Jordan.

A camel can tolerate an extraordinary degree of dehydration, losing well over a third of its body weight, and since it is very economical with water, it can manage longer without drinking water than any other domestic animal. The water is drawn from the tissues and cell fluids, while the blood serum remains almost constant and thus the circulation of the blood can continue without hindrance.

The animal can quench a moderate thirst (for a dromedary this is around 20 gallons (70–90 litres)) in one draught in barely ten minutes. When very thirsty it has to drink twice or three times in several hours, in order to make good the water it has lost.

The length of time camels can manage without water depends upon the air temperature, the kind, quantity and water content of their food, the type of pasture, the age and working capacity of the animal. Investigations carried out over a number of years on the food and water requirements of the free-grazing camels in the Sahara have shown that as long as the temperatures do not rise above about 104°F (40°C), the intervals between individual waterings are rather irregular. Even in high summer the herds left to themselves often drink less than is generally assumed. For example, in the Grand Erg Occidental (southern Algeria) with green shrub vegetation with maximum temperatures of 104–140°F (40–46°C) in the shade, they drink only every 4–7 days, a little more often on dry pastures. As soon as the nights become cooler, however, and the temperatures easily fall below 104°F (40°C), a camel can go up to 14 days without drinking. Even those animals which feed upon salt-loving plants in August, come to drink water only every 2–3 days when the temperature is about 104°F (40°C). They then consume enormous quantities at a time. The maximum is about 50 gallons (200 litres). Nevertheless, camels are, normally, extraordinarily moderate drinkers, since they drink only twice as much as human beings in the same area, that is, an average of 5–6 gallons (20–30 litres) each day. The water drunk is not stored, but is distributed all over the body within 48 hours.

In many regions of the Sahara the liquid obtained from plants lasts from October to April, on average pastures 2½–4 gallons (10–15 litres) a day is sufficient for requirements. At this time of the year no water is needed for heat regulation.

Camels are also very temperate in their eating habits. They can ingest about 100 lb (40–50 kg) of green fodder daily on succulent spring pastures, but if necessary they can go for months on 11 lb (5 kg) of straw a day. The average daily ration is 11–22 lb (5–10 kg) (dry weight). Nevertheless, they are rather 'choosy' about their food. They have, however, the useful characteristic that they always move about when feeding, in contrast

to goats which destroy everything. Thus camels instinctively guard against destroying the desert pastures. In order to maintain the nomadic life, which is the principal form of economy of the desert, the sources of water must be improved and multiplied.

The domesticated Two-humped camel has a more plump body and longer hair than the One-humped, particularly on the lower part of the neck and shoulders and on the head, humps and neck. It is usually a uniform dark brown in colour, but there are also white individuals. The Bactrian camel is very hardy in cold climates, has a thick winter fleece and a heavy moult. The area of distribution extends from southern Siberia and Manchuria through the whole of Central Asia as

Bactrian camel, two-humped Asian camel.

far as Asia Minor and southern Russia. It is chiefly used as a beast of burden by the nomads in the interior of Asia and can be found in latitudes up to 55°N (Omsk, Lake Baikal) and at altitudes up to 13,500 ft (4,000 m). Bactrian camels mate in the spring, even in zoos, and are the only Camelidae to keep to this season. The period of gestation is about 13 months (390–410 days).

Probably the earliest record of the domestic Bactrian camel dates from 3000 BC from western Turkestan and northern Iran, but the time and place of its first domestication have not yet been established.

The wild camels in the sandy and dusty deserts of Mongolia (Transaltai, Alachan Gobi) differ in their uniform desert colour (grey-ochre), thinner coat, small humps, weak development of the leg callosities and lack of chest callosity. They are said to live in groups of 5–12, to mate in February and drop their young in March. To what extent these are domestic camels which have long reverted to the wild, does not seem to be completely clear. FAMILY: Camelidae, ORDER: Tylopoda, CLASS: Mammalia.   H.G-P.

CAMELIDS, members of the family Camelidae, characterized by the possession of sole

pads, include two genera: the Old World species of *Camelus,* the Arabian and the Bactrian camels and the South American guanaco and vicuña, genus *Lama,* with the domesticated llama and alpaca.

The camelids differ from other hoofed animals in that the body load rests not on the hoofs but on the sole pads and only the front ends of the hoof touch the ground. The split upper lip, the long curved neck and the lack of tensor skin between thigh and body, in contrast to the horses and cattle, so that the legs look very long, are characteristics of these animals. They have no gall-bladder, go at an ambling pace like bears, giraffes and elephants, and are unique among mammals in having elliptical blood corpuscles. They all have an isolated upper incisor, which in the males of the *Lama* species is hooked and sharp-edged, like the tusk-like canines found in both jaws. These tusk-like teeth are a dangerous weapon and to some extent a substitute for the horns of most of the other ruminants.

The ancestors of the Camelidae must be sought in North America from where, towards the end of the Tertiary period, about two million years ago, one branch migrated across the Bering Straits into Eurasia. The other branch reached South America only in the Ice Age (Pleistocene) and gave rise to the present *Lama* species. In North America the camels died out towards the end of the Ice Age with the *Camelops* species.

All the camelids live in dry climates with great differences of temperature and high radiation intensity. They have a more or less great resistance to dehydration. They all live in very inhospitable regions, the Camelidae of the New World in the high mountains of the Andes, those of the Old World in desert and steppes, and they all serve peoples who live in ceaseless conflict with the forces of Nature.

The Camelidae are the only ungulates to pair in the recumbent position. The mothers do not free their young from the embryonic sheath nor do they lick them dry or eat the placenta. A few hours after birth the young are already suckling in a standing position after a brief search for the teats, and it is obvious they have the instinct to search in an angle approximately between vertical and horizontal. On the whole all the camelids have much the same motor patterns, some appearing spontaneously soon after birth (shaking, stretching, rolling over, stamping, etc.), others develop gradually (scratching themselves, nibbling, pawing the ground and all the forms of social behaviour).

While the two groups show different threatening attitudes, all the Camelidae show a similar behaviour when attacking: they run into their opponent broadside on, biting the legs, neck and throat (the body also in the case of *Camelus*) while at the same time pressing down the neck.

Distribution of camel family:
Bactrian camel, top right, Arabian
camel, bottom right; llama, top
left, alpaca, centre left, vicuña,
bottom left.

Many hornless ruminants fight thus. Members of the *Lama* species can also inflict deep wounds with their hooked tusk-like teeth. There is also the springing attack, more frequent with *Lama* than with *Camelus,* which is accompanied by snapping at the legs, lying over the standing foe and kneeling on the overthrown opponent, in order to squeeze him to death. It may happen, at least in camels, that both the embattled animals strangle each other simultaneously. There are also a number of approaches to the mating ritual. All stages of the fighting behaviour are already present in the young animals in their play-fighting, which is very intensive, particularly in the Camelidae of the New World. As they grow older, it more and more frequently becomes real fighting. The foals also play racing and mating games (riding each other) but they never play with inanimate objects, like many other ungulates. ORDER: Tylopoda, CLASS: Mammalia.   H.G-P.

CAMOUFLAGE, body colour and shape that hides an animal from its predators. The principles of camouflage are well exemplified by *cryptic colouration.

CANARY *Serinus canaria,* a finch named after the islands from which it was first brought, which has now been domesticated to become a common cage-bird. The wild bird is a subspecies of the European serin and is also found in the Azores and Madeira.

Canary, once universally popular cage bird, still has its place with specialist bird-fanciers.

3 Gloster canary. This is a new variety, similar to the Border, but smaller and slimmer, being about 4 in (10 cm) long. It includes a 'plain-headed' type, and a 'crested' type, in which the crown feathers are dark and fluffy, and radiate from a central point.

4 Yorkshire canary. This is a large, upright, rather carrot-shaped bird, about 7 in (18 cm) long, and usually colour-fed.

5 Norwich canary. A large, sluggish, heavily-built, almost spherical bird, it is about 6 in (16 cm) long, with a very broad head and soft copious plumage. 'Plain headed' and 'crested' varieties exist, in many colours. It is usually colour-fed and, when crossed with other finches, produces attractive infertile hybrids.

6 Red factor canary. This species has been developed in recent years, initially by crossing canaries with the Hooded siskin *Spinus cucullata* of South America. The offspring are fertile and richer in colour than other canaries. It is one of the most lightly-built varieties, unmarked and about 4 in (10 cm) in length, and is still being developed. FAMILY: Fringillidae, ORDER: Passeriformes, CLASS: Aves.   I.N.

CANDIRU or carnero, a small South American catfish which becomes parasitic on larger fish. Habitually it lives in the gill cavities, and with its sharp teeth and the spines on its gill covers it induces a flow of blood on which it feeds. The best known species and one that is greatly feared by the peoples of Brazil is *Vandellia cirrhosa*. This little fish enters the urinogenital apertures of men and women, particularly if they happen to urinate in the water. It seems likely that this is accidental, the fish mistaking the flow of urine for the exhalant stream of water from a fish's gills. Having penetrated, however, it is almost impossible to remove the candiru without surgery because of the erectile spines on the gill cover. The South American Indians often wear special sheaths of palm fibres to protect themselves. The candiru thus has the distinction of being the only vertebrate to parasitize man. FAMILY: Trichomycteridae, ORDER: Cypriniformes, CLASS: Pisces.

The male is a streaky olive-green above and yellow-green below, while the female is duller and browner. The bird was apparently brought to Germany early in the 16th century, and the modern yellow varieties have been developed by selective breeding from chance mutations. During domestication, the sexual dimorphism of the wild bird has also been lost, and now the only way of telling the sexes apart is by the song of the male, which is also more elaborate than in the wild bird. Yellow canaries come in pale and dark varieties. The former have less pigmented, longer, silkier feathers with white tips and are called 'buffs'; the darker ones have heavily-pigmented, shorter, coarser feathers, and are called 'yellows'. Streaky green, white, brownish, cinnamon and irregularly marked birds also occur, in which 'yellows' and 'buffs' are also distinguished on feather form, irrespective of their real colour. By adding red cayenne pepper to the diet during moult, a process called 'colour-feeding', the natural hues can be intensified, turning yellow birds almost orange. The following are the most common modern varieties, in all of which 'yellows' and 'buffs' are distinguished.

1 Roller canary. An old variety, about 4½ in (11 cm) long, bred primarily for its song. It was developed first in the Hartz mountains of Germany, but is now bred widely in

Europe and North America. Singing contests are held, in which the birds are judged on the quality and variety of their notes, the different phrases being given special names.

2 Border canary. This is the standard canary, compact, well-rounded, about 5 in (13 cm) long and available in a greater variety of colours than other types. This has long been the most popular variety in Britain, mainly because of its hardiness and the ease of breeding. It is not usually colour-fed.

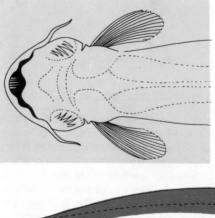

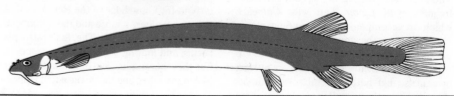

Candiru, a small South American catfish, liable to enter the urethra of river bathers. Spines on the gill-covers (see top drawing) makes its removal difficult and painful.

CANNIBALISM, the eating of other members of the species. There are no animals which consistently practise cannibalism. This in itself would obviously lead to the rapid extinction of the species. Nevertheless, many animals will on occasion eat the eggs, young or even adults of their own species. Usually this happens when population density is high resulting in over-crowding, but there are many instances of individuals turning on their own young for no apparent reason. Cannibalism, then, in the animal kingdom is as infrequent as in human societies.

The caterpillars of both Monarch and Queen butterflies will eat unhatched eggs voraciously for about six hours after they themselves have left their eggs. The more larvae there are in an area the greater is the percentage of eggs consumed, so destruction of them in this way is a density-dependant factor in the control of the population. Each species will consume the eggs of the other equally with their own; they do not discriminate when taking this kind of food.

Adult Flour beetles *Tribolium castaneum* will eat eggs they encounter as they move through the flour in which they live. As the number of beetles in a fixed volume of flour increases, more eggs will be laid and the likelihood of a beetle encountering an egg is greatly increased. Destruction of eggs is one of the factors which cause the initial increase in population density to flatten out as the progeny of a single pair of beetles put in a small quantity of flour multiply.

Crowding of adults often causes them to attack and eat each other. Scorpions kept in

Scorpion fly *Panorpa germanica*. After an unsuccessful courtship the female feeds on the male.

Green African praying mantis *Sphodromantis* female eats brown male who has tried to court her.

captivity will fight to the death, after which the victor eats the vanquished. In a cage this goes on until the number of scorpions is very much reduced. Even a plentiful supply of cockroaches as food does not alter this, if anything it makes matters worse for the scorpions fight over the prey. The more cover that is provided, however, the fewer animals will be killed.

When Spider crabs *Hyas araneus* are put in an aquarium they are hostile to each other from the start but are protected from attack by their thick exoskeleton. But for four days after moulting, during which their new outer covering is hardening, they are like all decapod crustaceans, very vulnerable. Unless a moulted crab is kept away from the others, it will be killed and eaten by its better-protected fellows. In the end only one crab is left in the tank.

Crowding of this sort violates the principle of individual distance and causes fighting. Under natural conditions, the crabs would be far enough apart for encounters to be avoided and they would be able to hide during their vulnerable period after the moult.

Complete breakdown of maternal behaviour can be seen when albino Norway rats *Rattus norvegicus* are over-crowded. The females leave their young about instead of preparing a nest and keeping them in it. These abandoned young ones are often eaten by adults. In addition some male rats will behave in a completely anti-social way, invading nests and eating the young. This can only be called pathological behaviour. Many instances of seabirds attacking and eating young in their breeding colony have been described. Terns, pelicans, and Man-o'-war birds have all been accused of this. Perhaps the most frequent offender is the Herring gull *Larus argentatus* which is commonly seen to kill young birds and eat them. But this behaviour is not confined to seabirds for heron, kestrel, wagtail, shrike and magpie have all been seen to consume nestlings. Very frequently young mammals are potential food for their own species; males of the vole *Microtus agrestis* are so likely to eat litters of young that in captivity the females must be isolated when about to give birth. If disturbed, female rabbits will eat their own young, indeed in one strain 8–15% of the litters suffered from cannibalism. Even young lions between nine months and two years of age may fall victim to other members of their species.

Possibly an explanation for this kind of behaviour can be found in a breakdown of the normal recognition processes by which food objects are recognized. These may be very delicately balanced to distinguish between young animals and potential prey; a very striking example of this is the behaviour of a mouth-breeding fish with a mouthful of young when it sees a worm. It will spit out the young,

take the worm, swallow it, and then suck the young back into its mouth. Clearly the worm is food and the young fish are to be protected, a differentiation which is carefully made in the animal's behaviour.

On occasion a female spider will devour the male which is courting her. Indeed in some species of spiders the male presents the female with food to hold her attention while he mates with her. It is difficult to see what biological advantage such destruction of the males may have. It is perhaps the Praying mantis *Mantis religiosa* which is proverbial for behaviour of this kind. Here the female insect decapitates her male partner, yet despite this copulation continues, indeed the headless body is unrestrained in its mating movements. This is evidence that the function of the brain is to inhibit activity; removal of the head lifts this inhibition so possibly cannibalism has a function at least in this case.

Except for such instances we can see this behaviour as the product of unnatural conditions of crowding and as a means by which population control is brought about.   J.D.C.

CANVASBACK *Aythya valisneria*, a duck of the pochard tribe Aythyini. It breeds in the western prairie provinces of Canada and west central United States and winters from British Columbia to Florida. FAMILY: Anatidae, ORDER: Anseriformes, CLASS: Aves.

CAPE HUNTING DOG *Lycaon pictus*, also known as the African wild dog. It ranges through Africa south of the Sahara. See dogs.

CAPE JUMPING HARE, one of several common names for a kangaroo-like rodent ranging over Africa south of the Sahara. See springhare.

CAPELIN *Mallotus villosus*, a small member of the salmon family from the northern Pacific coasts of North America and Asia. It is notable for the great shoals of adults that swim ashore to lay their eggs on the sand, the beach often being covered by masses of fish and eggs. A rather similar phenomenon is seen in the grunion *Leuresthes tenuis*, a small fish the life cycle of which is closely tied to the phases of the moon. The fishes swim as far up the beach as possible during high spring tides and bury their eggs in the sand; the eggs hatch and the larvae make their escape to the sea within a few minutes of the next high spring tide reaching them. FAMILY: Salmonidae, ORDER: Salmoniformes, CLASS: Pisces.

CAPERCAILLIE *Tetrao urogallus*, a large game bird of the grouse family, found in forests, particularly of conifers, in northern Europe and Asia, with a relict population in the Pyrenees. The cock capercaillie is very striking, some 34 in (86 cm) long, with a basically grey plumage, brown wing-coverts and dark glossy blue-green breast. The tail coverts and belly are marked with white and there is a white wing patch. The strong bill is dull white and there is a bright red wattle above each eye. The legs are feathered. The female, 24 in (61 cm) long, is cryptically coloured like other female game birds, mottled and barred with buff, grey and black.

Cock capercaille, dandy among gamebirds, in display attitude, challenging his rivals with song.

A typical example of camouflage, showing a hen capercaillie at her nest.

Capercaillies prefer dense, shady forests with substantial underbrush interspersed with glades and boggy areas. They feed on a variety of plant materials, particularly the buds and needles of pine, spruce and larch. This makes them unpopular with foresters, but a moderate population does little real harm. The flesh of the capercaillie is palatable and for centuries this species has been hunted for sport and food. This, with deforestation, brought about their extermination in Britain in the 16th century but re-introductions from 1837 onwards resulted in the species becoming re-established.

Cock capercaillies have a particularly striking breeding display. In the spring small numbers of cocks gather at the lek, or display ground, each beginning its display with a peculiar clicking utterance which develops to a crescendo and terminates with a loud 'pop', followed by a short wheezy, grating sound. The characteristic attitude during this song is with the neck stretched up to display beard-like feathers beneath the chin, with wings drooping to touch the ground and with the tail fanned and almost vertical. Noisy flapping of the wings and jumps into the air also take place. Rival males are charged, with the wings drooping, but most of the attacks are ritualized and seldom result in much injury. Occasionally, however, a particular male will attack moving objects other than its real rivals, including vehicles and humans, sometimes resulting in the death of the capercaillie.

The nest is usually on the ground, well hidden amongst the forest vegetation or under a fallen branch, frequently at the foot of a tree. 5–8 eggs are laid and incubated by the female for about 28 days. The eggs in any one clutch all hatch within a few hours, and the young are precocial, following the female and picking up a variety of plant and animal food for themselves. FAMILY: Tetraonidae, ORDER: Galliformes, CLASS: Aves.   P.M.D.

CAPILLARIES, extremely narrow, thin-walled blood vessels which connect the smallest arteries to the veins. Their walls are permeable to water, dissolved salts and other substances of low molecular weight, and the main exchange of such substances between the blood and the tissues occurs through the capillary walls.

CAPUCHIN, South American monkey so named because the hair on its head resembles the capuche or cowl of a Franciscan monk. It is the monkey formerly most favoured by organ-grinders. See New World monkeys.

CAPYBARA, similar in form to an over-grown Guinea pig, it is the largest of all living rodents, being the size of a sheep or a large dog. The two species, found in South America, belong to the genus *Hydrochoerus,* which is usually considered to be the sole member of the family Hydrochoeridae. However, this genus is sometimes placed in the family Caviidae which includes the Guinea pigs. A fully grown animal is about 4 ft (1·3 m) long with almost no tail and rather long legs. The unusually deep muzzle gives a very characteristic appearance and is correlated with the long, rootless, evergrowing cheek-teeth, four in each row, that are adapted for grinding tough vegetation. In size, structure and way of life capybaras tend to take the place of the herbivorous ungulates which are so poorly represented in South America. Capybaras are semi-aquatic and this is reflected in their partially webbed feet, sparse coat and the thick deposit of fat in the skin.

The best known species, *Hydrochoerus hydrochaeris,* is common and widespread in South America, being found in woodland adjacent to rivers, lakes and swamps from the Parana River in Argentina northwards. A smaller species, *H. isthmius,* occurs in Panama. Capybaras often live close to cultivated areas and sometimes damage crops of cereals and fruit, but their normal diet consists of aquatic vegetation and grasses.

They are sociable animals and it is not unusual to find a party of 10–20 feeding together in a weed-filled waterway at dawn or dusk. In the water they behave rather like hippopotamuses, swimming with only the tops of their heads or even only the nostrils exposed and readily submerging if they are disturbed. When resting on land they sit on their haunches like dogs.

Capybaras have only one litter of young each year. Gestation is about four months and usually about four or five rather well-developed young are born which can swim competently from an early age. They do well in captivity and can be seen in most zoos. FAMILY: Hydrochoeridae, ORDER: Rodentia, CLASS: Mammalia.   G.B.C.

Capybara or Water cavy, largest living rodent.

CARABAO, one of several common names for the Water buffalo *Bubalus bubalis.* See Bovidae.

CARACAL *Caracal caracal,* usually known as a lynx, but in fact more closely related to the serval, must surely be classed as one of the most beautiful of the cats, if not the most beautiful. It is long legged and is better adapted for running than most of the other cats, although it also shows remarkable agility and leaping ability. It is slightly smaller than the Jungle cat, measuring about $27\frac{1}{2}$ in (70 cm) and is much more slender. The colouring is a regular reddish brown above, with no other markings except for the ears, which are black behind, and a small dark spot above each eye. The underparts are white, with vague brownish red spots on the belly. The tail is short and the ears have distinctive tufts or plumes at their tips.

The caracal is widely distributed throughout the drier areas of southern Africa and Asia and, although it was formerly much more common than it is now, it can still be found throughout its former range. While the caracal prefers open country, it will also be found in mountainous areas, bush and desert. For the most part, it is semi-nocturnal and prefers to lie up during the day in hollows, under tree roots or even in a disused porcupine or aardvark den.

The main food source of the caracal is birds, which the cat hunts when they are roosting, although it has been observed to catch some prey when it was on the wing. An indication of the strength of this cat is that it is known to kill and devour the strong Martial eagle, among others. In addition to eating birds, the caracal will take quite a wide range of small animals such as duiker, steinbok, sheep, goats, and even young reedbuck and impala. The caracal's system of hunting is very similar to that of a leopard and involves a stalk and then a light-pounce. It is a good climber, which has obvious advantages for capturing roosting birds, although it has not helped the survival of the species when being pursued by man, as the cat will climb a tree if pressed by dogs and this makes it all too easy to shoot.

There is really very little known about this attractive cat, but we do know that the size of the litters varies between one and three, with a maximum of four and an average of two. The young resemble the adults at birth, and the majority of breeding occurs in July and August.

Although these animals give an impression of great ferocity, they can be trained and have been in India since ancient times. They used to be kept by the wealthy for the hunting of other animals in much the same way as the cheetah has been trained. In some areas the caracal was much prized and was kept and trained to compete in the catching of pigeons. FAMILY: Felidae, ORDER: Carnivora, CLASS: Mammalia.   N.J.C.

CARACARAS, large, long-legged carrion-eating birds of the sub-family Daptriinae, belonging to the falcon family, Falconidae, but looking quite unlike true falcons. Found commonly in parts of South and Central America, caracaras associate with vultures at carcasses, but some are insectivorous or omnivorous. They build their own nests, unlike true falcons, but will rob other car-

rion-eaters of their food. They are well adapted for walking and running and live in forests, savannah, or more open country. There are four genera. See also vultures. FAMILY: Falconidae, ORDER: Falconiformes, CLASS: Aves.

CARAPACE, the dorsal or upper half of a turtle's shell. It is connected to the ventral or lower half, or plastron by a bony 'bridge'. The carapace is comprised of nearly fused ribs and bony plates that are essentially forced into shape during a period of rapid embryonic growth. The bony plates of the carapace are covered with shields or scutes of a horn-like substance. These overlying shields, which also provide colour and pattern to the shell, have little relationship to the arrangement of the underlying bony plates. The shields, useful in identification, have specific names. Those down the centre of the back are vertebrals, on either side the costals, and those along the edges are marginals. Some species have a small shield centred on the anterior or front edge called the nuchal.

The word is also used for the chitinous covering on the backs of other animals, especially of crustaceans.

Cardinalfish *Apogon nematopleris.*

CARDINALFISHES, a family of small marine fishes mainly from the tropical Atlantic and Indo-Pacific, although a few species enter freshwater. They have two dorsal fins, the first spiny, and two spines at the front of the anal fin. Most species are only a few inches long. Some have luminous organs and many species brood the eggs in the mouth. *Apogon endekataenia* lives amongst the spines of certain long-spined Sea urchins while *A. stellatus* lives in the mantle cavity of giant conch shells. In *A. ellioti* there is a luminous gland near the front of the abdominal cavity. The light is provided by cultures of luminous bacteria and the photophore or light organ has a lens and reflector. Two more photophores are found near the end of the intestine. The muscles surrounding

the anterior photophore are translucent and it is they that act as the lens.

Cardinalfishes are often extremely numerous. Professor W. Gosline reported catching over 1,000 specimens of a 3 in (8 cm) species, *A. brachygrammus,* within a very small area of the reef.

The cardinalfishes are predominantly brown and red in colour. In those species that care for the eggs, it is sometimes the male that takes the eggs into the mouth and sometimes the female. FAMILY: Apogonidae, ORDER: Perciformes, CLASS: Pisces.

CARDINALS, a name given to some birds with red plumage and, by association, transferred to other similar or related forms.

In North America the name 'cardinal' is usually applied to a large, heavy-billed bunting *Pyrrhuloxia (Richmondena) cardinalis,* also known at times as the 'redbird'. The male is almost entirely red save for a black patch on the throat, and has a small spiky erectile crest. The female is similar but mostly brown, with only a little red in the plumage. A related cardinal, *P. phoenicea,* a little less vivid in colour, occurs in northwestern South America. These birds are members of the subfamily, Pyrrhuloxinae, which are known as cardinals or cardinal-grosbeaks.

The cardinal-grosbeaks include the most colourful seed-eaters in America, males being brightly coloured although the females are usually brown. The males of the genus *Passerina* are variously deep blue, light blue and buff, blue, scarlet and green, purple, red and blue and blue, green and yellow. The male is deep blue and buff in the Blue grosbeak *Guiraca caerulea* and black and white with a red breast patch in the Rose-breasted grosbeak *Pheucticus ludovicianus.* Other species are more drab. The pyrrhuloxia *P. sinuata* is grey and red with a slender crest and a heavy parrot-like bill. These heavy bills are used for seed-eating, although insects and some fruit are taken. The thrush-sized saltators of Central and South America have large but less stout bills and are better adapted to fruit- and plant-eating. They are rather dull-coloured birds with yellow, white and black head markings. The cardinal-grosbeaks are mostly woodland birds, usually occurring in pairs but sometimes flocking when not breeding. As a group they have loud melodious songs, mostly of rather short phrases and usually delivered from a conspicuous perch. They make typical cup-shaped nests in trees or bushes at varying heights from the ground. The eggs are variously coloured but usually spotted or blotched, although some saltator eggs are blue with a tight wreath of fine black lines around one end. The female incubates but the male helps with the care of the young.

Caracal or Desert lynx, now almost extinct.

Male cardinal *Pyrrhuloxia cardinalis*.

The name cardinal is also applied to some South American species of true bunting, Emberizinae. The Dominican cardinal *Paroaria coronata* is smaller than the North American cardinal but has a similar crest. Its red colour is limited to the head and throat, the rest of the plumage being black, grey and white. Four other species of this genus are also called cardinals and resemble the Dominican cardinal in colour but lack the pointed crest. Another species is the Green cardinal *Gubernatrix cristata*. This is larger than the others and is olive-green with blackish streaks, a black throat, and yellow streaks on the head of the male and whitish streaks on that of the female. Both sexes have a pointed black crest and it is probably this, by analogy with the North American bird, which has given these others the name 'cardinal' since the Black-crested finch *Lophospingus pusillus* of South America, a small grey bird with a black and white head and pointed crest, is sometimes called the Pygmy cardinal. Another cardinal is the fodi *Foudia madagascariensis,* of Madagascar. This is a weaver the male of which is scarlet except for dark wings and tail and a few black streaks on the back during the breeding season. The female is streaky brown. It is a bird of savannahs, sociable when not breeding, and constructing the typical domed, pendent weaverbird nest in a tree. ORDER: Passeriformes, CLASS: Aves.

Young bull Barren ground caribou, Alaska.

CARDISOMA, a tropical genus of Land crabs, which cause great damage to rice cultivations by undermining the banks impounding the water in the paddy fields. See Land crabs.

CARIBOU *Rangifer tarandus,* a large rather ungainly looking deer of the tundra and northern forest regions. It has a wide distribution in both eastern and western hemispheres, being referred to as reindeer in the east and caribou in North America.

In the eastern hemisphere, two mainland and one insular races of reindeer occur. The European tundra reindeer *R. t. tarandus* is found in parts of Scandinavia and Russia, where it continues its range eastwards into Siberia north of about latitude 65°N as far as Yakutsk. Further south it is replaced by the woodland type reindeer, *R. t. fennicus,* the range of which extends from Karelia into eastern Siberia as far as Kamchatka and northern Mongolia and Manchuria. A third race, *R. t. platyrhynchus* occurs on the islands of the Spitsbergen archipelago.

In the western hemisphere two types of caribou—the Barren-ground and the Woodland caribou—are recognized, their range including much of Canada and adjacent northern islands and Greenland. About 150 animals of the woodland type still remain in the United States, the majority of which are found in northern Idaho, the remainder being in Washington State. The word 'caribou' is the North American Indian's name for this deer, which was also formerly described as *Maccaribo.* Four subspecies of Barren-ground and two Woodland caribou are recognized in North America.

The bulls have a thick muzzle, maned neck and broad flat hooves that are concave

underneath and designed for travelling over snow and boggy terrain. The bulls are considerably larger than the cows, but both sexes of caribou are larger than the reindeer of northern Europe and Siberia. A full-grown caribou bull will vary in height at the shoulder from about 42 in (107 cm) to just over 50 in (127 cm) according to the subspecies, whilst the weight will vary from 200 lb (91 kg) to 600 lb (272 kg). A full-grown European reindeer bull will measure 44–45 in (112–114 cm) at the shoulder, the cows being some 4–6 in (10–15 cm) less. The largest animals would appear to come from north British Columbia.

The body colour of the adult males is brown, with the neck a palish grey turning white in winter. There is more variation of colour in the female, particularly in reindeer which have been domesticated.

As with moose and elk, it is customary to refer to the sexes as bulls and cows rather than stags and hinds, or bucks and does, which is normal with other species of deer. Females of both reindeer and caribou are unique in normally possessing a pair of antlers, similar in construction to, but considerably smaller than those of the males. The bulls generally have a palmated 'shovel' close to the face on one of the antlers, although a shovel on each of the antlers is by no means a rarity. The upper points are also frequently palmated and there is a back tine about halfway up the main beam. A common belief is that this shovel is used to dig through the snow to enable the deer to reach the lichen underneath. This is not true, for throughout most of the winter the older bulls will be without antlers and the forefeet are used to paw through the snow. The antlers on the older males are shed during the early

Barren ground caribou on high snow patch for relief from flies (Denali in background). Mt. McKinley National Park, Alaska.

part of the winter, but the new growth does not commence until the spring. The younger animals retain their antlers until the early part of the year, but not until late spring or early summer, at about the time the calves are being born, are the cows' antlers cast. A good pair of Scandinavian antlers will measure about 50 in (127 cm) in length, but North American heads may be up to 8 or 10 in (20–25 cm) longer.

This deer is usually silent, and even during the rut, which takes place in late September–October, the bulls utter no special challenge call. The calves are born in late May and June.

The caribou is a gregarious animal and is usually to be found in herds which are small except during the long migrations of spring and early winter, when they may run into thousands.

Although the lichen *Cladonia rangiferina* forms the staple diet many other forms of willow, mosses, grasses and sedges etc. are eaten with relish.

Of all the species of deer, the reindeer has been the most utilized by man, and in Scandinavia there are probably more 'domestic' reindeer than wild ones—indeed there are no truly wild ones left in Sweden today. To the Lapps of Scandinavia and tribes of northern USSR the reindeer is indispensible, for it is the basis of existence for these nomadic people, providing food, clothing and transport. The caribou has not been so domesticated, but domestic reindeer from Scandinavia have been introduced to Alaska and northern Canada. FAMILY: Cervidae, ORDER: Artiodactyla, CLASS: Mammalia.
G.K.W.

CARINATE, the state of possessing a carina, or keel, on the sternum, in birds. The carina serves for the attachment of the flight muscles and is therefore typical of the flying birds as opposed to the flightless, or *'ratite', birds. The term 'carinate' can also be used to designate a bird possessing a carina, that is any bird not a ratite.

CARNIVORA, an order of mammals characterized by the basic equipment of a flesh-eating mode of existence: large canine teeth, reduced and pointed cheekteeth, and sharp claws on all the toes. Some members of the order, however, have ceased to be carnivorous in their diet, and have a secondary series of herbivorous characters overlaid on their carnivorous ones: the bears, and most particularly the Giant panda *Ailuropoda,* are prime examples of this.

Carnivores vary in size from the $1\frac{1}{2}$ oz (40 gm) of the smaller weasels to the 1,770 lb (800 kg) of the largest bears. The fast-moving true carnivores, such as dogs and cats, are digitigrade; the ponderous, more vegetarian bears are plantigrade. Claws are retractile in most of the cats, and semi-retractile in the civet-group; such claws are more curved and sharper than in dogs or bears.

The teeth are highly specialized in carnivores, most markedly in the cats which are the acme of carnivore evolution. The dental formula is, varying according to family and genus, $\frac{3.1.2-4.1-2}{3.1.2-4.1-3}$. Incisors are somewhat reduced, especially in the lower jaw, and used mainly for holding prey. I^3 is the largest of the upper series. Canines are very large, curved and dagger-like and are generally the main despatching weapon. Cheekteeth, almost always reduced in size as well as number, are pointed, with high sharp cusps. P^4 and M_1 alone are unreduced, in most forms, and work together as a shearing instrument. They are known as carnassials and, like most of the highest carnivore specializations, are most strongly developed in cats.

Meat is an extremely simple substance to digest, being in the readily usable form of animal protein. Consequently the alimentary canal is unspecialized. Not only is there little need for salivary digestion (hence the reduced cheekteeth of which not even the carnassials have a masticatory function), but later stages of digestion and absorption are also uncomplicated. The stomach is simple. The caecum is small or absent and the whole intestine averages only three to four times the length of the trunk, compared to man in which it is at least five times as long. In herbivores it can be as much as eight to ten times as long as the trunk.

Carnivores do not, by and large, lie in wait and jump on their prey; hunting includes a phase, however short, of running. A lion will make a short dash from cover and attempt to pull down prey that will only be some 20 ft (6 m) away. The Canidae (dog family) on the other hand hunt in packs and chasing is the major part of the hunt. Accordingly the limbs are adapted for running:

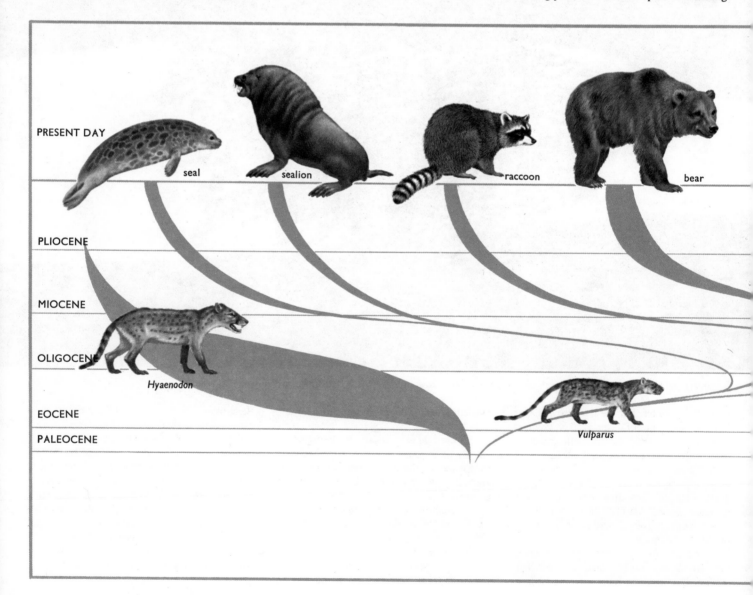

PRESENT DAY

seal   sealion   raccoon   bear

PLIOCENE

MIOCENE

OLIGOCENE

Hyaenodon

Vulparus

EOCENE

PALEOCENE

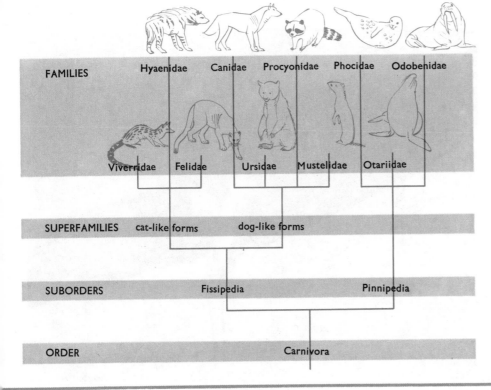

the clavicle is reduced or absent and limb movements are restricted to a backward and forward motion. Whereas ungulates, which are equally built for running, need a strong, well-knit leg, the use of the claws in carnivores demands that some mobility be retained in the rotatory action of the limbs. Therefore, in contradistinction to the ungulates, the tibia and fibula are not fused, nor are the radius and ulna. In the wrist there is some fusion of elements: the scaphoid and lunate bones are fused and the centrale is absent. Five toes are found on all four feet of bears, procyonids, mustelids, the aardwolf and most viverrids; four in dogs, hyaenas and cats.

Carnivores have large brains and generally emerge as intelligent creatures when

(Above) Schematic representation of the classification of the Carnivora, and (below) the evolution of the order in relation to the geological succession.

tested. The reasons for this are quite clear: flexibility is an important part of their behaviour, both because of the variety of prey species on which most carnivores rely, and the variety of conditions under which they must catch their prey. Learning plays an important part in their development, and the young are born blind and helpless (although not naked), and spend a long time in complete dependence on their mothers. Their play while young, for which they are noted along with Primates, is directed towards hunting techniques and manoeuvres. Young felids will ultimately accompany their mothers on hunts, and learn to stalk and kill from her. Gradually she begins to let them kill for themselves, and the long-drawn-out and inefficient killing, which looks so disgusting to the human eye, is in fact a vital stage in the maturation of the young lion or tiger.

Nor do adult carnivores necessarily kill very cleanly. Most canids hunt in packs and run their prey in relay until it is exhausted and as soon as, and often before, it has collapsed on the ground, a dozen snapping jaws are tearing it to pieces. The 'clean swift kill' formerly considered typical of the Felidae has been found by Schaller and others to be largely a matter of luck. Killing may take the form of neck-breaking with a hard blow, or of slowly choking by hanging onto the prey's neck.

Although most species of carnivores avoid complete dependence on a single form of prey, there is always a preferred 'prey size' and a few species which are especially sought. The lion concentrates on prey of an approximately similar body weight to itself, such as large antelope or zebra; leopards prey on baboons, wild pig, small antelope or deer, usually smaller than themselves; the tiny weasels and stoats prey on creatures much larger than themselves. Finally, as has been remarked already, some members of the order have become predominantly vegetarian in diet.

In their mode of reproduction, carnivores differ little from most other mammals. They have a vascular type of penis, like all mammals except the Artiodactyla and Cetacea, but in some forms, especially dogs and bears, the baculum is so large that most of the erectile tissue is crowded out. This leads to a condition in which the penis cannot be extracted from the engorged vulva for a matter of minutes or hours after copulation, and the partners remain linked—the 'mating tie' familiar to dog-breeders. Except for a few forms with a small baculum, such as the panda, a mating tie is found in all Canidae, Ursidae and Procyonidae.

Carnivora generally have multiple births, with litters of from 2–12, or more. Mammae are numerous, three pairs at least, and abdominal. Mortality within a litter is very

Leopard *Panthera pardus* with antelope kill, which it has carried up the tree to eat undisturbed.

Skull, hindlimb and forepaw of the four main groups of the Carnivora.

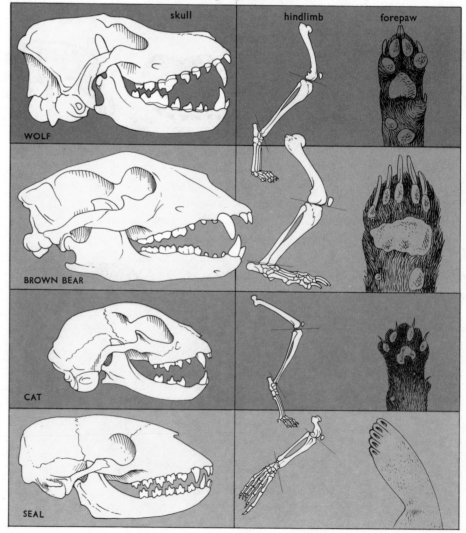

high, and as often as not only a single survivor reaches maturity. Both monoestrous and polyoestrous forms occur—usually the former are canoids, the latter feloids—and other reproductive anomalies are found. Mustelidae show delayed implantation, making the gestation period appear longer than it actually is as do some Ursidae, while Canidae may have a prolonged pseudopregnancy, with lactation etc., when they are not impregnated after oestrus.

Living land carnivores are divided into eight families in two superfamilies, as follows:

Superfamily Canoidea	
Family Canidae	Dogs, foxes
Ursidae	Bears
Procyonidae	Raccoons, kinkajou etc.
Mustelidae	Weasels, badgers, otters etc.

Superfamily Feloidea	
Family Viverridae	Civets, mongooses
Hyaenidae	Hyaenas
Protelidae	Aardwolf
Felidae	Cats

In the Canoidea the sense of smell, important in all carnivores, is enhanced by the enlargement of the maxillo-turbinals, an arrangement of intricate, scroll-like bones on the floor of the nasal cavity. In the Feloidea the ethmo-turbinals, which are derived from the ethmoid bone further back and higher in the nasal cavity, are enlarged at the expense of the maxillo-turbinals and push forward to the anterior end of the nasal cavity. Whether this has any profound effect on olfaction is unknown, but it may indicate that the two groups have independently come to rely on their sense of smell.

Another difference between the two is in the structure of the basicranium. In the canoids the paroccipital processes are prominent and well separated from the auditory bulla, while in the feloids they are not so prominent, and are in direct contact with the bulla. The bulla itself differs in structure. In the Canoidea it is derived from the tympanic bone, but in the Feloidea from both tympanic and entotympanic, and the two portions (when both are fully ossified, which is not always the case) are separated by a partition.

Finally the two groups differ in the male reproductive organs. In the Canoidea Cowper's glands are present, and the bulla is very large in most cases, while in the Feloidea, Cowper's glands are absent and the bulla is small.

There are a number of problems connected with the classification of the Carnivora. The number of families is by no means settled. On behavioural grounds the mongoose group shows sufficient differences

from the civet group to rank as a separate family (Herpestidae) according to some. Another of the Viverridae, the fossa (*Cryptoprocta*) appears to be very primitive in some respects, and it has been suggested that it in fact would be better placed in the Felidae. The classification of the Felidae is also a matter for dispute. The cheetah (*Acinonyx*) is universally recognized as a good genus which probably belongs in a subfamily of its own, but among the other cats as many as 15, or as few as one, genera have been recognized. The aardwolf (*Proteles*) is still placed by some authors in the Hyaenidae. It shows such numerous differences and such contrary specializations, however (although it is likely that it has evolved quite recently from the hyaena group), as to make an inclusive 'Hyaenidae' almost indefinable. The hyaena jaw is modified for crushing bones and is enormously strong with well-developed carnassials. The aardwolf in contrast feeds on ants, and has small, reduced, spaced teeth, none of which can be called carnassials, and very weak jaws.

Within the Canoidea the most difficult problem concerns the position of the pandas, the Giant panda *Ailuropoda* and the Lesser or Red panda *Ailurus*. The latter has nearly always been placed in the Procyonidae, a family otherwise restricted to the New World. When the Giant panda was discovered, the similarity in its colour-pattern and teeth to the Lesser panda raised questions of its possible inclusion in the Procyonidae, but other anatomical features, as well as its general form and appearance, seemed to align it with the bears (Ursidae). The late D. Dwight Davis, who went into the matter in depth, pointed out that the classification of the Giant panda seems to have been a matter of geography and linguistics. Anglo-American authors almost without exception would assign it to the Procyonidae, specialists on the continent of Europe, to the Ursidae. Some also would place the Giant panda, with or without the Lesser panda, in a separate family altogether.

Davis's conclusions, arrived at after dissections, study of osteological material, and consideration of all available evidence, are as follows: (1) *Ailuropoda* belongs to the Ursidae. (2) 'Ignoring minor polishing effects', the differences between the Giant panda and other Ursidae amount mainly to changes in the masticatory apparatus (larger and more complex cheekteeth, increased mass of bone tissue in the skull, elevation of mandibular articulation above the toothrow level and enlarged masticatory musculature), associated with the completely herbivorous diet. (3) *Ailurus* is not closely related to *Ailuropoda* but is closest to the Procyonidae. For a number of reasons it makes an un-

Small clawed otter *Amblonyx cinerea*, of India.

Feline genet *Genetta genetta*, eating small bird.

Weasel *Mustela nivalis* and prey (a Wood mouse).

satisfactory procyonid but nevertheless it is, at present, best included there. (4) The resemblances between the Procyonidae and the Giant panda are due to convergence in diet, not to primitive retention, since the Procyonidae and Ursidae are independently derived from canid ancestors.

The Giant panda is the most completely herbivorous of all the order Carnivora. In the wild it is said to feed almost entirely on bamboo, although in captivity it can be persuaded to take other foods. It is not at all surprising that the Ursidae and Procyonidae, the two carnivore families with the most pronounced tendency towards a herbivorous diet, should have produced forms so closely paralleling one another in the specializations of the masticatory apparatus.

Probably the most thorny problem facing carnivore specialists today is the question of the phylogeny of the Pinnipedia. This group, the marine carnivores (seals, sealions and walruses), have sometimes been placed in an order by themselves, sometimes in a suborder of Carnivora, but several authors have recently suggested that they are diphyletic and not a natural group at all. The seals (Phocidae) are considered to be descended from the Mustelidae, and some authors even specify from the Lutrinae, the subfamily of Mustelidae which includes the otters, while the Otariidae (sealions) and Odobaenidae (walruses) are thought to have emerged from the Ursidae. The evidence for this traditionally depends on skull structure, especially in the basicranial region. More recently serological techniques have been brought to bear on the question, and seem mainly to confirm the suspected diphyly. I. A. McLaren has attempted to establish two fossil carnivores, *Potamotherium* and *Semantor*, as serially intermediate between Lutrinae and seals. Morphologically there are grounds for this, but neither genus is adequately placed stratigraphically, the latter being thought to be Upper Miocene (and hence possibly contemporaneous with the earliest seals) while the former is only known to be 'Tertiary'.

The pinniped question has an obvious bearing on the classification of the carnivores in general. For the moment, however, the marine carnivores are left in their traditional place, and only the land carnivores are treated in the present article. It may be noted, however, that the Ursidae are among the most aquatic of 'land carnivores' and the Polar bear *Thalarctos* for example is largely marine, while the highly aquatic Lutrinae have at least one fully marine representative, the Sea otter *Enhydra*.

Carnivores are economically more important than is generally realized. Not only do most families (especially the Mustelidae and Felidae) include valuable fur-bearing species, which have, in characteristic human fashion, been grossly overexploited, some to the very brink of extinction, but in their position at the top of many food-chains they perform an essential function in pest-control. Bounty systems and extermination campaigns against carnivores have inevitably resulted in the discovery that a predator's function in controlling deer, rodents, monkeys and other agricultural pests far outweighs its destruction of occasional items of livestock, and that its conservation is a vital necessity if man and nature are to continue to coexist.   C.P.G.

CARNIVORES, animals which feed exclusively, or virtually exclusively upon other forms of animal life and in so doing cause the death of their individual prey. They range in size from tiny spiders to lions and tigers. They form the higher links in any food chain and species feeding in this way are found in every phylum of the animal kingdom.

CARNOSAURS, a group of large bipedal carnivorous dinosaurs belonging to the order Saurischia. They were the dominant predators of the Jurassic and Cretaceous periods and represent the largest land predators in the earth's history. They had a world-wide distribution but their numbers were small judging by the scarcity of their fossils. The main organ of predation was the massive head carried on the short and powerful neck. The jaws were set with a battery of dagger-like teeth. The carnosaur forelimb underwent progressive reduction and was all but vestigial in advanced forms like *Tyrannosaurus*.

CARPET SHARKS, a family of moderately sized but occasionally large sharks characterized by a prominent groove running from each corner of the mouth forward to the nostril where there is a thick and fleshy barbel. Other fleshy appendages are often found around the margin of the head and these, together with the mottled or marbled body colours, help to conceal the fish against the background of the seabed. There are two dorsal fins and, unlike most sharks, the tail is not turned upwards but continues the general line of the body. The Carpet sharks are also unusual in that they show habits transitional between the oviparous or egg-laying sharks and the ovoviviparous or live-bearing sharks. Members of the genera *Stegostoma*, *Nebrius*, *Chiloscyllium*, *Hemiscyllium* and *Parascyllium* lay eggs, while live young are produced by species of *Ginglymostoma*, *Orectolobus* and *Brachyaeturus*. There are between 20 and 30 species of Carpet sharks, all from the Indo-Pacific area except the Atlantic Nurse shark *Ginglymostoma cirratum*. The latter is one of the largest members of this family, reaching 14 ft (4·2 m) in length, and it occurs in tropical waters on both sides of the Atlantic. The Zebra shark *Stegostoma fasciatum* of the Pacific is another large species (up to 11 ft or 3·3 m) and is recognizable by the dark stripes on the body. The majority of sharks are rather nondescript in their colouration, but the Carpet sharks are exceptional and especially in the case of the species from Australian waters, where they are known as 'wobbegongs'. In these the body is marked with green, brown and white and the colour pattern is so striking that their skins have been tanned for leather. The Carpet sharks feed on a variety of invertebrates (prawns, lobsters, cuttlefish, Sea urchins) and also on fishes. Two or three rows of teeth are usually functional in each jaw. In spite of their sometimes large size, the Carpet sharks are not aggressive but have been known to use their teeth in defence. FAMILY: Orectolobidae, ORDER: Pleurotremata, CLASS: Chondrichthyes.

CARPET VIPERS *Echis,* a genus of the viper family with two species living in the deserts and semi-deserts of northern Africa and Arabia and in the western and southwestern parts of Asia. They are strongly venomous and have the reputation of striking without provocation. *E. carinatus* throws its body into coils and, by moving adjacent coils in opposite directions, rubs them together to give a loud rasping sound. FAMILY: Viperidae, ORDER: Squamata, CLASS: Reptilia.

CARPS or carp-like fishes, slender streamlined fishes almost entirely found in freshwater, although a few will occasionally go

Carpet shark
Orectolobus barbatus.

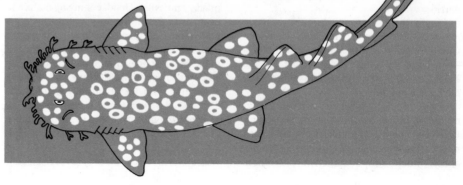

Japanese Hi-goi or Golden carp.

rulers urging them to improve the supply of carp for the king's table.

The carp-like fishes are all egg layers. The so-called Viviparous barb *Barbus viviparus* was at first thought to produce live young (like the toothcarps) but it is now known to reproduce like other cyprinids. Some species lay eggs in shallow water, some in deep, some attach their eggs to aquatic plants, while yet others release their eggs into the water so that they float downstream with the current while the embryos develop. In tropical countries the period of embryonic development may be very short, the larvae hatching in only 36 hours. Other species, such as the bitterling, have formed strange associations with other animals for the care of their eggs.

There are 14 species of carp-like fishes in Great Britain, many of them meriting a separate entry (see barbel, bream, bleak, chub, dace, gudgeon, minnow, roach, rudd, tench and White bream). All of these are also found on the continent of Europe and a few, such as the roach and the minnow, reach right across to Asia. The slow spread of the carp-like fishes from Asia is shown by the fact that there are many more species in Asia than

Crucian carp.

into brackish water, as in the Baltic Sea. Their main centre of distribution is southern Asia from whence they may have originally evolved. Carp-like fishes are entirely absent from South America, Australia and also Madagascar, which was isolated from the mainland before the carps entered Africa. In South America, the ecological niches normally occupied by carps are taken by the related ostariophysin family of Characidae (which may have been ancestral to the Cyprinidae).

Typically, the carps are fairly slender, with silvery scales, a single dorsal fin set at about the midpoint of the body and a forked caudal fin. There are no teeth in the jaws, but these may develop a horny cutting edge for scraping algae or may bear disc-like lips which act as a sucker. One or two pairs of short barbels may be present at the corners of the mouth. Mastication of food, such as insects, plants, detritus, is achieved by a set of teeth in the throat, the pharyngeal teeth (see separate entry). Identification of these fishes is often extremely difficult, especially those in Africa and parts of Asia about which little has been recorded and the collections of which in museums are small. In many cases, the description of their colours in life has had to wait until quite recently when certain species have become better known through the efforts of aquarists.

The larger carp-like fishes have long been an important source of food in inland areas. As a result, some have been artificially introduced into many parts of Europe, North

America and certain tropical countries, sometimes to the detriment of the indigenous species. The Common carp *Cyprinus carpio* is a native of Asia but was introduced into England via Europe, presumably by monks who kept these fishes in monastery tanks, in about the 12th century.

In Ethiopia a scaleless domesticated variety of the Common carp has recently been found and this too must have been an introduction and is thought to have been brought in by Italians in 1942. The Crucian carp *Carassius carassius,* a close relative of the goldfish, is a native of Asia and Europe that was introduced into England in about the 17th century. There was an interesting report from Essen in 1806 of a Crucian carp found inside a hailstone, but clearly this is not a normal method of introduction. The Common carp is now widespread in the United States and its introduction dates from fishes imported into California from Germany in the 1870s. Conditions in America seem to suit it and a magnificent specimen of 55 lb (25 kg) has been recorded from American waters. Wild goldfish, which escaped from ponds and aquaria, have now become established in some parts of America. In Japan, the Common carp has for centuries been regarded as a symbol of fertility, but the earliest record of this fish is from China in 500 BC. The first European record seems to be that of Theodoric (475–526 AD), King of the Ostrogoths, whose secretary Cassiderus was compelled to issue a circular to provincial

in Europe, more in Europe than in England and more in England than Ireland, to which island very many of the species never reached before it separated from the mainland. The European forms show a number of interesting adaptations. The rapfen is unusual in having an underslung lower jaw and predacious habits. The bream, the White bream and the vimba are highly flattened (laterally compressed) forms, a body shape that gives them great manoeuverability. The zeige *Pelecus cultratus,* an insectivorous and surface-living form, is very similar in appearance and habits to the Asiatic genus *Culter* (the two genera are fairly closely related). Other European forms are adapted to life in swift streams, for example the gudgeon, or to still waters, for example the tench. Finally, there are many

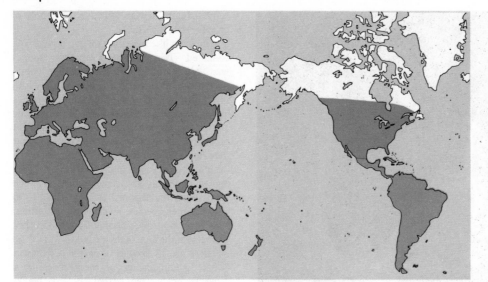

Distribution of the Cyprinidae or carp-like fishes (purple), absent in the yellow regions.

more generalized forms, typified by the minnow *Phoxinus phoxinus*.

The Common carp is a moderately deep, laterally compressed fish with a large dorsal fin, short anal fin and two pairs of barbels round the mouth. The scales in wild carp are large, there being about 35–37 along the lateral line, but in the domesticated varieties there are either just a few large scattered scales (Mirror carp) or no scales at all (Leather carp). Carp are very commonly used in fish culture, especially in eastern Europe. By breeding resistant strains, it has been possible to grow them near to the Arctic Circle as well as under tropical conditions. The Common carp grows to a large size and, in addition to the American record already quoted, an English specimen weighed 44 lb (20 kg) and one from South Africa weighed no less than 85 lb (40 kg). Carp are hardy fishes and in winter tend to form shoals of 50 or more which cluster together in the deep waters of lakes or ponds. At this time their metabolic rate drops sharply so that they can be said to 'hibernate', although it is now more usual to speak of this as 'winter torpidity'.

The Near East represents a zone of mixing, with carp-like fishes derived from the European, African and Asiatic faunas. Few of the genera are limited solely to this region, but the genus *Cyprinion,* a form in which scales are lacking, probably has the centre of its distribution in the Near East, as may the minnow-like *Phoxinellus.* The shoaling cyprinid *Acanthobrama* of Lake Galilee could have been the fish that accounted for the 'miraculous draught of fishes' recorded in the Gospels. *Acanthobrama* swims in large shoals near the surface and such shoals can be seen at some distance by anyone standing in a boat or on the shore.

As might be expected, the carp-like fishes

of the Asiatic continent are numerous and very diverse. They range in size from the small barbs and danios, which may mature at only a few inches, to the huge mahseer of India which reaches 9 ft (2·7 m). In *Osteochilus* of the East Indies the lower jaw projects as a sharp edge beyond the upper, the mouth being directed upwards and fringed by papillae. In Lake Tung Ting in China there is a predacious cyprinid, *Luciobrama macrocephalus,* that has evolved the pike-like body typical of lurking predators that make a

sudden lunge towards their prey. Other carp-like fishes are adapted to the torrential streams of the Himalayas. The majority, however, live in rivers, streams and lakes and provide a most important source of food in inland areas.

The carp-like fishes of Africa are clearly derived from immigrants that made their way to the continent from Asia. Genera such as *Barbus, Labeo* and *Garra* are common to both Africa and the southern parts of Asia, including the Near East. In the rivers of Africa, the carp-like fishes have had to compete with the characins and catfishes, and in the lakes they have had to contend with the very numerous species of cichlids. Perhaps as a result of this, there are fewer genera than in Asia. The genus *Barbus* includes many species, of which a few grow to a length of 18 in (46 cm) or more and form the basis for important fisheries in the rivers and lakes. *Labeo* spp., with soft, underslung jaws, and *Varicorhinus* spp., with scraping jaws, are widespread. In species of the genus *Garra* the mouth is bordered by disc-like lips for attaching to stones in fast streams, while the pectoral and pelvic fins are set low on the body to provide greater friction against rocks (a form of specialization most highly developed in the Hillstream fishes—see separate entry). Rather primitive in appearance, the species of *Barilius* take the place of the minnow in African waters. One of the most

Common carp of Europe.

The Mirror carp, a domesticated variety of the Common carp, is named for the large scales on its flanks.

surprising adaptations is found in *Caecobarbus* spp., the Blind barbs of the Congo. After the great lake fisheries for cichlids, the carp-like fishes are next in importance as a source of food in many of the African territories.

The carps of North America share few genera with Asia. They appear to have entered the continent from the northwest via the Bering Bridge and from the few forms that did this have evolved the present-day American cyprinids. Strictly speaking, *Catostomus* and the other American suckers should be dealt with separately since they belong to the family Catostomidae, but it is more convenient to mention them here because they are closely related to the cyprinids and share many features. As their name implies, they have protrusile, sucking mouths. There are a few Asiatic species, mainly in eastern USSR, and these are more generalized in form than the American species.

The White sucker *Catostomus commersonii* is extremely widespread in North America, being found throughout Canada and as far south as Mexico. Like most suckers, it is not brightly coloured. It reaches about 6 lb (2·7 kg) in weight, as also does the Long-nose sucker *Catostomus catostomus*. The latter supports a commercial fishery on Lake Superior, where it is found at depths of 600 ft (180 m). The Quillback sucker *Carpoides cyprinus* can be easily identified by its highly flattened (laterally compressed) body and the elongation of the first few dorsal rays, from which it gets its name. The largest of all the suckers is the Bigmouth buffalo sucker *Ictiobus cyprinellus*. Average specimens weigh about 3 lb (1·4 kg), but the record fish (from Spirit Lake, Iowa) weighed over 80 lb (36 kg). The Buffalo sucker differs from other members of the family by having a terminal mouth, that is at the end of the snout and not underneath. As a result, it can make use of a much more varied

diet. Seeds of plants are often eaten, and in Iowa these fishes eat the 'cotton' from the cottonwood trees in springtime. Small fishes are also taken. The Humpback sucker *Xyrauchen texanus* from the Colorado river shows an interesting parallel with one of the few Chinese suckers, *Myxocyprinus asiaticus*. Both fishes are very deep-bodied, a shape usually evolved in fishes that live in still waters, and one that presents serious problems in fast rivers. In each case the fishes have, so to speak, solved the problem in the same way. The body is not the same thickness at the top and the bottom but is sharply keeled along the high back. Water streaming past the fish tends to force it closer to the bottom where presumably the fish finds it easier to keep its station against the flow of water. One other species deserves mention, the Northern hogsucker *Hypentelium nigricans* of the United States. This species has the more usual dorso-ventral flattening of the body found in fishes that live in fast water. It frequently enjoys the company of trout which swim after it eating the insect larvae that it dislodges while it roots around stones at the bottom.

The other large group of American carp-like fishes are those referred to as minnows, although they are often large and are not closely related to the European minnows. Often called dace, chub or shiners, they will be dealt with under the heading minnows.

As one of the principal freshwater groups of fishes, it is natural that the cyprinids should provide many of our commonest aquarium fishes. The vast majority of those imported by dealers come from India and the Far East, although some of the African species are becoming popular. Details of some of these are given under barbs and danios and a quick glance at the number of *Barbus* species now available in pet shops shows something of the success of this genus in the tropics. An unusual member of this group is the so-called Flying barb *Esomus danrica* from India,

Ceylon, Thailand and Singapore. This is a slim, silvery fish with a red and violet iridescent sheen. One pair of barbels are extremely long and reach back to the midpoint of the body. Its common name alludes to its very large pectoral fins, but although these fishes are prone to leaping, there is no evidence that they actually 'fly'.

The widespread genus *Labeo* provides many aquarium fishes from India and Southeast Asia. In *Labeo* the mouth is ventral, lying under the snout, and the lips form a sucking disc lined with sharp, horny ridges. *Labeo bicolor*, known as the Red-tailed black shark, has a velvety black body, dorsal, anal and pelvic fins, while the caudal fin is a vivid red. The species is easy to keep provided that soft, peaty water and plenty of shade are available. It grows to at least 6 in (15 cm) and, although an algal feeder, will happily accept lettuce leaves as a substitute. While kindly disposed to other fishes, it is advisable not to have more than one large specimen in a tank since they tend to attack members of their own species. The Black shark *Morulius chrysophekadion*, a close relative of *Labeo bicolor*, is jet black with a faint red or yellow spot on each scale and a large dorsal fin. It grows to 22 in (56 cm) in the wild. Another species that is often imported is *Labeo frenatus*, a peaceable fish with a brown body and pale red fins.

The genus *Rasbora* is widespread throughout east and south Asia and is common on many of the islands of the Indo-Malayan Archipelago. The rasboras are mostly shoaling fishes with slim bodies, one of the few exceptions being the deep-bodied harlequinfish. The Brilliant rasbora *Rasbora einthoveni*, from Thailand and the Malayan islands, has a yellow-olive back and flanks with a bluish sheen on which runs a shining band of black, dark green or emerald from the snout to the base of the tail. The Pigmy rasbora *R. maculata*, from southern Malaya, is a tiny species which reaches only 1 in (2·5 cm) in length. The body is red to yellow (redder in males than females) with dark blotches at the base of the fins. The Scissortail *R. trilineata* receives its name from its habit of closing the forks of the tail as it swims, the movement being made more obvious by the black band on either lobe of the otherwise colourless tail. FAMILY: Cyprinidae, ORDER: Cypriniformes, CLASS: Pisces.

CARRION BEETLES, large beetles feeding on decaying animal matter. Over 200 species of Carrion beetles have been described. The true Roving carrion beetles *Silpha* are dark coloured, broad bodied and rather flat. Other species called Burying beetles *Necrophorus* are frequently strikingly marked with orange or yellow and black. They are known for their habit of excavating soil from under the bodies of small mammals and birds, so that these drop into the earth and are buried. The larvae of *Necrophorus* feed on the decaying corpse and in combination with Roving carrion beetles, fly maggots and bacteria, rapidly reduce it to skin and bone. FAMILY: Silphidae, ORDER: Coleoptera, CLASS: Insecta, PHYLUM: Arthropoda.

CARTILAGE or 'gristle', forms the skeletal material of the embryos of vertebrates and of the adults of a few groups, and covers the articular joint-surfaces between limb bones. It is formed by secretion from rounded connective tissue cells known as chondrocytes, and includes both gel and fibrous elements.

The gel is translucent and firm but elastic. It does not contain blood-vessels, since substances can diffuse to and from the chondrocytes through the cartilage.

Due to the lack of any rigid element, cartilage can grow not only by addition at its surface but also (unlike bone) by internal expansion. This expansion gradually separates the chondrocytes, but these may then subdivide to form new cells. The outer surface of a cartilaginous element is covered by a layer of dense connective tissue, and it is to this that tendons and ligaments may be attached.

During early development in vertebrates, the deeper-lying bones of the skeleton appear first in a cartilaginous form, and this is later replaced in most of them by bone. Only in the cyclostomes (lampreys and hagfishes) and cartilaginous fishes is cartilage retained as the skeleton of the adult, and in the cartilaginous fishes it is often strengthened by the deposition of calcium salts.

A thin film of cartilage normally provides the smooth joint-surfaces between limb bones. Erosion of this surface may occur in the painful disease known as arthritis. Cartilage also forms the discs which separate the bodies of the vertebrae, and the flexible basis of the external ear in mammals.   C.B.C.

CARTILAGINOUS FISHES, members of the class Chondrichthyes which includes the sharks, rays and chimaeras as well as certain fossil fishes.

CASSIOPEIA, a sluggish jellyfish which lives upside-down on the floors of shallow lagoons in warm tropical seas and is particularly common around Florida and the West Indies. The bell of the jellyfish is firm concave, on the side nearest the seabed, with a raised ridge round the margin by which it adheres to the bottom. There are eight branching 'mouth-arms' bearing 'suctorial mouths'. However, food organisms are taken in by the action of flagella. The bell pulsates and this creates water currents which bring food and oxygen to the sedentary jellyfish. The life-history is known and the ciliated planula larva develops into a scyphistoma, similar to that found in other jellyfish. Ephyrae, small *medusae, are produced by transverse fission of the scyphistoma but only one ephyra is produced at a time. This has a scalloped edge to the bell with 16 sense tentacles. The young medusa possesses a typical four-lobed mouth, characteristic of the Scyphozoa, but as it grows the lobes become divided and the edges join over to form the grooves of the 'mouth-arms'. See Cnidaria and scyphistoma. ORDER: Rhizostomae, CLASS: Scyphozoa, PHYLUM: Cnidaria.

CASSOWARIES, large flightless birds of the genus *Casuarius,* living in the tropical rain-forests of New Guinea and adjacent islands and in northern Australia. Three species are recognized in the most recent statement of the classification of the family Casuariidae, to which cassowaries belong. and these birds, together with the one species

Section of cartilage showing groups of cells.

Cassiopeia, the upside-down jellyfish.

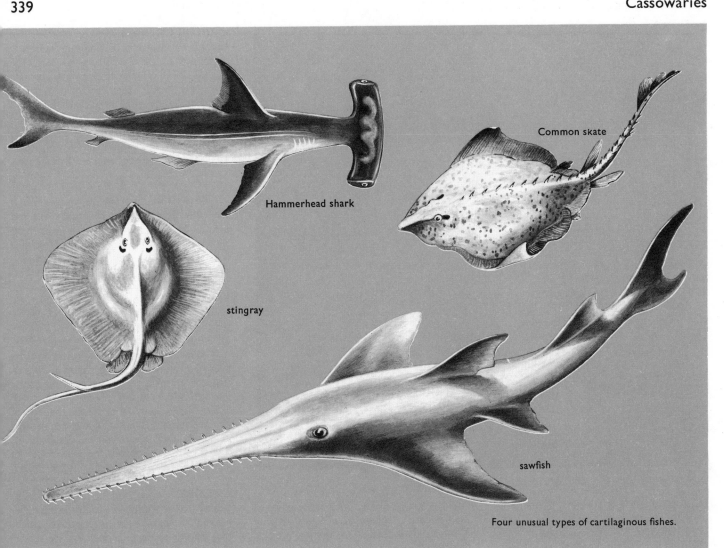

Common skate

Hammerhead shark

stingray

sawfish

Four unusual types of cartilaginous fishes.

of emu *Dromaius* are the only living members of the order Casuariiformes. Although the Casuariiformes are recognized as *ratite birds, there is little agreement about their relationships to other ratite groups.

Adults of the largest, the Double-wattled cassowary *Casuarius casuarius,* stand about 6 ft (1·8 m) high when erect, but normally the head is held about 4 ft (1·2 m) above the ground. The body is shorter than that of the emu, and the bird appears stockier. The plumage is almost black and has a glossy texture. Each feather has two equal shafts, and as there are no barbules the barbs of the feathers do not link together to form a firm vane. The plumage hangs loosely from the body looking more like hair than feathers. The head is embellished by a casque, or flattened horny crown, projecting up to 6 in (15 cm) above the top of the skull. The skin of the head and neck is blue, and in two of the three species ornate wattles, or folds of loose skin coloured red, orange and yellow, hang from the neck over the throat. The cassowaries have three toes, flattened beneath as in the emu, with a long sharp claw on the innermost toe of each foot.

The bill is narrower than the emu's and perhaps a little longer. The wings are greatly reduced and the wing quills, of which only the shaft is present, are horny spines, up to 15 in (38 cm) long, which hang conspicuously at the bird's side as it stands.

The Double-wattled cassowary lives mainly in the rain-forests of New Guinea and the surrounding islands, as well as northeast Australia, as far south as Cardwell. At least in New Guinea its habitat extends into savannah forest (eucalypt forest). It has two large wattles, about $5\frac{1}{2}$ in (12 cm) long, hanging from its neck. The casque of this species often leans to the left.

The Single-wattled cassowary *C. unappendiculatus* stands 5 ft (1·6 m) tall and weighs up to 128 lb (58 kg). It lives in riverine and coastal swamp forests of New Guinea and adjacent islands. Its single wattle is only about $1\frac{1}{2}$ in (3 cm) long and hangs from the throat.

The Dwarf cassowary *C. bennetti* is considerably smaller than the others, standing about $3\frac{1}{2}$ ft (1 m) high, and inhabits montane forests in most parts of New Guinea and the surrounding islands. Although a few popu-

lations are found in lowland forests, it is generally uncommon below 3,500 ft (1,000 m) but may be found up to 10,000 ft (3,000 m). Its population is nowhere as dense as the lowland species. The plumage of the Dwarf cassowary is silky but duller than the other species, and it has no wattles. All three species are broken into numerous subspecies, but many of these are founded upon single specimens, or on the colours of the soft parts, which are now known to be very variable even within a single population.

Very little has been recorded about the biology of any of the cassowaries. There are a few casual observations made by residents of and visitors to North Queensland, and some useful information has been collected by various expeditions to New Guinea. The birds appear to live in pairs and family parties, each pair defending a territory during the breeding season. Eggs are laid from May onwards, and have been found even in September in North Queensland. Incubation probably takes about seven weeks, and in captive birds the male undertakes the whole of the incubation, as in the emu. The clutches so far recorded range from three to eight

Double-wattled cassowary, the commonest of the three species.

eggs and the nest is a scrape on the forest floor in the dense vegetation of the bird's normal habitat. The chicks are striped with a dark and light longitudinal pattern and probably resemble those of the emu. There is no information about the rate of growth, but it is clear that the juvenile plumage is brown and the ornamental wattles do not appear until the young bird matures, probably during its second or third year.

Wild cassowaries have been recorded eating the fruit of various native and cultivated plants throughout the year, and swallowing whole items as bulky as a large plum. Leaves have also been found in their gizzards, but it is likely that other plant, and probably animal, food is taken at times when fruit is in short supply. They appear to be good swimmers and have frequently been seen bathing. The calls have been differently transcribed by various observers, but there appear to be two main types. All observers record a throbbing type reminiscent of the emu's drumming, and a call reminiscent of emu grunting has been heard just prior to breeding.

New Guinea natives capture the chicks and rear them until they are large enough to eat, and also pluck feathers from their captives to use in their ornamental head-dresses. Captive and cornered cassowaries have a reputation for attacking humans and several

fatalities have recently been reported from New Guinea. They apparently use the long claw on their innermost toe in these attacks, throwing both legs forward together as they jump at their opponent.

So little is known about the field populations of these birds that it is impossible to gauge whether any of them are in danger of extinction. It is, however, clear that the Dwarf and Single-wattled cassowaries live at lower population densities than the Double-wattled cassowary. FAMILY: Casuariidae, ORDER: Casuariiformes, CLASS: Aves.
S.J.J.F.D.

CASSOWARY CLASSIFICATION. The Keram people of New Guinea class cassowaries in a group of their own, *kobity*, rather than in *yakt*, the birds and bats. The reason given is that cassowaries have no feathers (the plumage being hair-like) and have bony skulls unlike the thin skulls of birds. Furthermore, the Keram say that cassowaries have a special relation with man. They must be killed with blunt instruments and the heart must be eaten to ensure that the spirit returns to the forest. Blunt instruments are considered essential for fighting relatives and when a man is killed, the heart of a pig is eaten as a substitute by the killer.

CASTOR OIL FISH *Ruvettus pretiosus,* an oceanic fish related to the Snake mackerels. It is known to the Spanish as escolar. The Castor oil fish is found in deep waters in most parts of the world, usually occurring at depths of about 2,400 ft (700 m). It reaches 6 ft (1·8 m) in length and the flesh is extremely oily and has purgative properties, hence the common name (true castor oil comes from a plant). FAMILY: Gempylidae, ORDER: Perciformes, CLASS: Pisces.

CATADROMOUS FISHES, species which pass downstream from freshwaters into the sea to breed, a good example being the freshwater eel. The majority of eels inhabit tropical waters but the anguillids (the freshwater eel and its relatives) and also the congrids (Conger eels) are exceptional in living in temperate waters. However, both groups make a fairly long migration between the feeding and the breeding grounds which are in tropical waters. It would seem, therefore, that the delicate eggs and larvae have been tied to the ancestral breeding areas and that any extension in the range of the fishes has involved only the larger juveniles and adults. One can infer, therefore, that fishes that are catadromous have evolved in the sea and have only later colonized freshwaters. The reverse is probably the case with the anadromous fishes.

CATBIRDS, name used for several different kinds of birds with calls which resemble the mewing of a cat. The other characters which they appear to have in common are rather dull plumage and a tendency to remain hidden in the cover of vegetation. In Australasia the name is usually given to two bowerbirds of the genus *Ailuroedus* which occur in the forests of northeastern Australia and in New Guinea. These are heavily-built with greenish, mottled plumage, and unusual because they do not make bowers and the male assists in the nesting in the more usual

Common catbird of North America.

passerine fashion. Their calls have been compared to the mewing of a cat and to a child crying. The Stagemaker bowerbird *Scenopoetes dentirostris,* of Queensland, a similar species which makes a leaf-strewn 'stage' for its performances, is sometimes called the Toothbilled catbird, the 'tooth' on the bill being used for snipping off the leaves that decorate its display ground.

In Africa there is the Abyssinian catbird *Parophasma galinieri,* small, dull, with some dark mottling on the head and rufous under-tail coverts. It is a skulking, little-known mountain bird inhabiting thickets at high altitudes. It appears to be mainly insectivorous, but its other habits are unknown. Its affinities are uncertain and it has been variously regarded as a babbler or

flycatcher. There is no clear indication why it should have been given the name 'catbird' since it is said to have a loud ringing call and varied song; but it may be from its superficial similarity to the North American species of that name.

In America two species of the mockingbird family are called catbirds. The best known is the Common catbird *Dumetella carolinensis,*

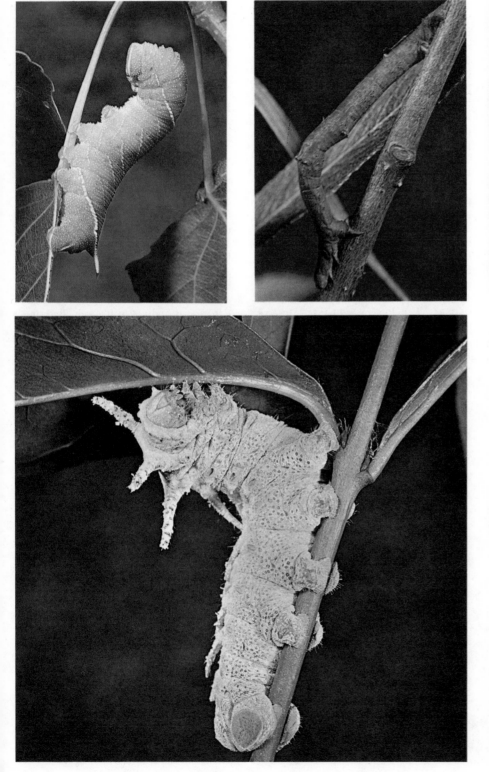

Caterpillar of Eyed hawkmoth *Smerinthus ocellatus* (top left), Looper caterpillar (Geometridae) (top centre), Lobster moth caterpillar *Stauropus fagi* (top right), Atlas moth caterpillar *Attacus atlas* (left).

of southern Canada and the United States. This species is dark slate-grey with a black cap, dull brown in young birds, and chestnut-red under-tail coverts. A Black catbird *Melanoptila glabrirostris,* similar to the other but with a glossy black plumage, occurs in Yucatan. These birds, little more than sparrow-sized but with a slender body and longish tail that is frequently flicked, are skulkers, associated with thick cover through which they slink. The Common catbird's call is a plaintive, cat-like mew, but it also has a prolonged and varied song, in which it may at times mimic other species. Its food is mainly insects, but it also takes some small, soft fruits. It builds a bulky cup-shaped nest of a variety of materials, which is usually well-concealed in the cover of thick bushes or creepers at varying heights. The eggs are glossy greenish-blue, rarely spotted, and are incubated by the female alone. Two broods may be reared in a season. ORDER: Passeriforms, CLASS: Aves.

CATERPILLAR, one of the four stages through which butterflies and moths pass in their life-histories: the other three being the egg, chrysalis and the perfect, and nearly always winged, form, the imago. The caterpillar develops between the egg and chrysalis stages and is most often worm-like in shape, possessing features characteristic of the ancient types from which the Lepidoptera (butterflies and moths) are derived. They have no wings or scales and the eyes, instead of being 'compound' as they are in the imago, are 'simple'; that is they possess a single lens, instead of numerous lenses each. Except for the shape of the legs, there is little external distinction between the thorax and abdomen, and the long antennae, so characteristic of the adult butterfly, are not evident. Moreover, the mouthparts possess the powerful biting jaws found so widely in insects and lack the tube, the proboscis, up which the adult butterfly or moth can suck liquid. Yet many of these features are, in fact, foreshadowed in the caterpillar. The wings have already begun to form in little pockets hidden under the skin, while structures exist in the mouthparts from which the proboscis is derived. The antennae are present though they are so small that a lens is needed to detect them. In those moths (the 'swifts') which are among the least highly evolved, the antennae are also minute.

The caterpillar usually casts its hard skin four times and it is only then, when the newly formed skin is soft and pliable, that the creature can effectively grow. It may change greatly in appearance on these occasions, for the protective devices appropriate to a very small animal, about $\frac{1}{10}$ in ($2\frac{1}{2}$ mm) long, are not always suited to a much larger one of about 4 in (10 cm) in length.

Many caterpillars at first live together in company, often within a web spun upon the leaves which they eat. This habit may persist or the individuals may scatter as they become older and use up their food supply. Although generally vegetarians, caterpillars often have cannibalistic tendencies, attacking others of their own, or of a different, species—but not if they are living in company.

Caterpillars are sometimes protected by a repulsive smell. This would be weak, probably useless, in so small a creature as a single newly hatched individual but is evident when a number congregate. Many caterpillars being hairy are avoided by most predacious birds with the exception of the cuckoo for instance. In some species, the colour-pattern matches their background to perfection, for example Brussels lace *Cleora lichenaria* bears an extraordinary resemblance to a twig covered with lichen. There are instances also, in which caterpillars acquire relative immunity through an alarming appearance. Caterpillars of the Elephant hawk *Deilephila elpenor* swell out their front segments when danger threatens, throwing into prominence the eye-like spots, making the caterpillar look like a small snake. To man, caterpillars are important as the source of genuine commercial silks, and also as the cause of much damage to crops. See Lepidoptera and moths.
ORDER: Lepidoptera, CLASS: Insecta, PHYLUM: Arthropoda. E.B.F.

CATFISHES, widespread chiefly freshwater fishes with barbels round the mouth. There are 31 families from all parts of the world except the colder regions of the northern hemisphere. Some have completely naked, scaleless bodies while others have a heavy armour of bony plates. There is a single dorsal fin followed by an adipose fin (see separate entry) which in some families (e.g. armoured catfishes) is supported by a spine. The common name for these fishes refers to the barbels round the mouth which look like whiskers and serve a sensory function in detecting food. Anatomically, the catfishes are interesting since the bones of the upper jaw (premaxilla and maxilla) have, to varying degrees, been reduced or are even absent. Where present they form a basal support for a pair of barbels. The vast majority of catfishes are found in freshwaters but two families are marine.

Europe has only two catfishes, both of which spread into Europe from Asia after the last Ice Age but which never reached the British Isles. The larger of the two, and one of the largest of the European freshwater fishes, is the wels *Silurus glanis* which is also found in Asiatic USSR. The second is *Parasilurus aristotelis,* an Asiatic species that is found in a few rivers in Greece. It was named after Aristotle whose very accurate account of its biology was doubted for 2,000 years until it was realized that his descriptions referred to *Parasilurus* and not to the wels. Both these catfishes belong to the family Siluridae the members of which are found across Asia south of latitude 40°N and north of the Himalayas to Thailand. The silurids are naked catfishes with the dorsal and adipose fins short, small or even absent. The anal fin may be very long and may be continuous with the tail. The Glass catfish *Kryptopterus bicirrhus* from Burma is familiar to aquarists. The body is completely transparent and slightly yellow and the dorsal fin is reduced to a single ray. There is a single pair of long barbels. In the aquarium, these fishes are peaceful and thrive on live foods but several individuals should be kept since solitary fish appear to become 'unhappy'. This species grows to about 4 in (10 cm) in length. The young of *Ompok bimaculatus* are also transparent and might be mistaken for the Glass catfish except that there are several rays in the dorsal fin. In the wild, it grows to 16 in (40 cm) and loses its transparency, but it stays much smaller than this in an aquarium. This fish is usually imported and sold in mistake for the Glass catfish.

In the southern part of its range the Siluridae overlaps with another family of naked catfishes, the Bagridae. In this family

The capitane, a naked catfish, showing fishes ascending the walls of a pothole in Colombia. The fishes move by alternate use of the sucker-like mouth (S) and the suction pad formed by the pelvic fins (P).

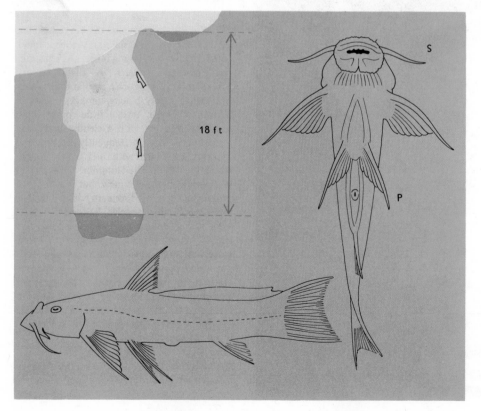

Caterpillar of American moth *Automeris* sp, bearing bunches of stinging spines that burn and irritate the skin of anyone handling them.

the dorsal fin is preceded by a stout spine, an adipose fin is always present and the anal fin is usually short. The family ranges through Asia Minor to south and east Asia, Africa, Japan and Malaysia. Many of the species of *Bagrus* in Africa grow up to 3 ft (90 cm) and are important in local fisheries. The genus *Leiocassis* from Thailand and Malaya contains several species commonly imported into Europe and the United States for aquarists. *Leiocassis siamensis* has a thick-set dark brown or blue-grey body with four irregular pale yellow vertical bands. *Leiocassis poecilopterus,* sometimes called the Bumblebee fish, has a brown-blue body with irregular yellow blotches. Both these species adopt the most unlikely resting positions, sometimes almost vertical. *Mystus tengara,* from northern India, has a greenish-yellow body with a brown back. The young are amenable to life in a community tank but the adults are liable to become predacious.

The family Ictaluridae contains freshwater catfishes from North America and Southeast Asia. The ictalurids have a naked body and a large head. In the United States they are called Tadpole madtoms or bullheads and are suitable for cold water aquaria (some have been introduced into Europe). These American catfishes are discussed under madtoms.

The family Schilbeidae contains Asiatic and African catfishes which resemble the silurids except that the dorsal fin has a sharp spine and the anal fin is very long. Members of the genera *Schilbe* and *Eutropius* of Africa are important elements in freshwater fisheries and are known as butterfish. The genera *Physailia* and *Paralia* contain species which resemble the Glass catfish in having almost transparent bodies, at least when young, and very long barbels. *Pangasianodon gigas* from Thailand is one of the largest of all the catfishes, reaching $7\frac{1}{2}$ ft (2·2 m) and like the wels has been thought to be responsible for the disappearance of small children.

The Clariidae have the same range as the schilbeids (Asia and Africa). They are naked, often elongated, bottom-living forms with cylindrical bodies and flat heads. Characteristic of this family is the possession of an accessory breathing organ in the form of blind sacs extending along the sides of the vertebral column from the top of the gill cavity or occurring as spongy tissue in the gill cavity (see air-breathing fishes). The dorsal and the anal fins are long and the adipose fin is small or absent. These are very voracious feeders, some growing to a length of 3 ft (90 cm) and forming important elements in fisheries. The genus *Clarias* is widespread and contains species which sometimes migrate overland at night. *Heterobranchus longifilus* from Africa, like several other catfishes, has very sharp spines in the pectoral fin which are capable of injecting poison and causing a most painful

Glass catfish or Ghost fish hovering among plants.

The pectoral girdle (P) and the pectoral spines (S) in a catfish to show the way the spines can be erected (right side of picture) and then locked in that position.

wound. *Heteropneustes fossilis* from India is commonly kept in aquaria when small.

The African family Mochokidae contains one of the best known of all the catfishes, the famous Upside-down catfish *Synodontis nigriventris.* The body is naked, an adipose fin is present, and there is a strong spine in both dorsal and pectoral fins. This fish has the habit of swimming on its back, with the belly uppermost, a habit that is, however, shared with a few other members of this genus. In most fishes the back is much darker coloured than the belly, but in *S. nigriventris,* as its Latin name suggests, the belly is darker than the back. This reversal of the normal pattern of counter-shading is a clear indication that this type of camouflage is of value to the fish. This species, which reaches 12 in (30 cm) in the wild, does well in an aquarium, remaining small, but it is liable to uproot the vegetation.

Species of *Synodontis,* like certain other catfishes, have an ingenious mechanism whereby the spines of the dorsal and pectoral fins can be locked when erect and in some the spines can inflict a painful, stinging wound. *Synodontis angelicus* from West Africa is one of the prettiest species, with round white spots on an intense red-violet background.

The family Chacidae from India and Burma contains only a few species. *Chaca chaca* grows to about 8 in (20 cm) in length and has an extremely flat body and a large head. It lives on the bottom and is beautifully camouflaged with blotchy dark browns and small protuberances to break the outline of the fish. So confident is it in its camouflage that it rarely moves even if touched, lying on the bottom like a piece of dead wood.

The South American family Pimelodidae is related to the rather similar Bagridae of the Old World. *Pimelodus clarias* has a grey-blue body with dark spots but should be handled with care since the dorsal and pectoral spines are capable of causing blood poisoning. *Sorubim lima* from the Amazon has a very flat head and a spatulate snout which overhangs the mouth. This lengthening of the snout is taken a step further in the Tiger catfish *Pseudoplatystoma fasciatum,* found from Venezuela to Uruguay, in which there is a very long, flat snout with three pairs of barbels round the mouth. This family also contains, like the Bagridae, species which are referred to as Bumblebee catfishes, for example species of *Microglanis* which are covered in yellow markings. *Typhlobagrus kronei* is a blind, cave-dwelling species from the Caverna das Areias, São Paolo, Brazil.

Upside-down catfish, of Africa, lacks the silver belly usual in fishes that swim the right way up.

Living at the surface in this same area is a normal species, *Pimelodella transitoria*, from which the blind form may have evolved.

Perhaps the most curious of the South American catfish families is the Trichomycteridae which contains the parasitic forms. One of these, the *candiru, is the only vertebrate parasite of man. *Stegophilus insidiosus* is a small, worm-like catfish that lives in the gill chambers of armoured catfishes. A second rather unpleasant South American family is the Cetopsidae which contains the genus *Cetopsis*. These repulsive, flaccid catfishes live in the upper reaches of the Amazon and feed on offal. They have a naked, slimy body and small eyes.

The family Aspredinidae contains the Banjo catfishes (*Bunocephalus*) the large round head and slender body of which has earned it its common name. Some members of this nocturnal family have developed ingenious methods of egg protection and incubation. In *Aspredinichthys tibicen* from the Guianas the female develops spongy tentacles on the belly during the breeding season, to which the eggs become attached. Most members of this family are from freshwater but a few species of *Aspredinichthys* venture into the sea.

Two of the South American families of armoured catfishes are very well known to aquarists. These are the Callichthyidae and the Loricariidae. The first is found throughout the tropical part of South America and in Trinidad. In these fishes the flanks are covered by two rows of bony plates and the adipose fin is preceded by a spine. They live in small shoals in slow-flowing water and grub around for food. The pectoral fins are provided with strong spines which are used in some species to help them move overland when the ground is moist and the air humid. Since the water in which they live is often foul and depleted of oxygen, the ability to breath air by taking it into the intestine enables the fishes both to survive the dry seasons and to make overland journeys. These are hardy fishes, well suited to life in an aquarium, where they undertake the important task of clearing up food from the bottom of the tank. The genus *Corydoras* is probably the best known of this family. *Corydoras paleatus* was one of the first of these catfishes to be imported into Europe, not later than 1878. It reaches about 3 in (7·5 cm) in length and has a brown to olive green body with darker spots and marblings. The Bronze catfish *C. aeneus* has a bronze-green body with a dark patch on the shoulder. *C. melanostictus* goes under a variety of common names (Pepper catfish, Leopard catfish, etc.) which refer to the many small brown spots on the pinkish flanks. Also called the Leopard catfish is *C. julii*. These and the many other species of *Corydoras* grow to about 3 in (7·5 cm) long, but the Dwarf corydoras *C. hastatus* is minute, reaching only 1 in (2·5 cm). Unlike the others it swims in midwater and rests on leaves of water plants. *Callichthys callichthys* is much larger, reaching 6 in (16 cm) in length. This species builds a kind of bubble nest under the leaves of floating plants and the male guards the eggs, grunting if disturbed. Species of *Hoplosternum* build similar nests, which may be strengthened with pieces of plants.

The distribution of the family Loricariidae is similar to that of the callichthyids. The loricariids are depressed, flattened forms with sucking mouths and three or four rows of plates along the flanks. Some species pass into brackish water, while the powerful sucking mouth enables others to live in mountain torrents, where they cling to stones with their sucker mouths while rasping away at algae with their jaws. The genera *Plecostomus*, *Otocinclus* and *Loricaria* are kept by aquarists primarily to keep down algal growth on the sides of the tank. In *Xenocara* the body is very depressed and there are twig-like processes on the snout and shorter spine-like processes on the cheeks. *Plecostomus plecostomus* and *P. commersoni* have the same flattened shape but lack the outgrowths on the snout and cheeks and have large, flag-like dorsal fins. Rarely growing to more than 6 in (15 cm) in aquaria, they reach 2 ft (60 cm) in the wild and are valued for food by the local people, who shoot at the fish with bows and arrows as they browse in shallow water. Large museum specimens of *Plecostomus* often bear telltale arrow holes. Members of the genus *Farlowella* have extremely thin bodies with long, slender snouts, giving them a passing resemblance to small twigs in the water. The whip-tail *Loricaria filamentosa* has the uppermost ray of the tailfin elongated into a filament. Members of this genus are flattened, bottom-living forms with bony plates not only on the flanks but also on the belly. This would appear to provide protection, but the author once made the mistake of keeping a 6 in (15 cm) whip-tail in an aquarium with two small piranhas of only 1½ in (4 cm) long. On one occasion the food for the piranhas was forgotten and the following morning only the tail of the whip-tail remained! Species of *Otocinclus,* and especially *O. affinis,* grow to 2–3 in (5–7 cm) and are placid, long-lived aquarium fishes.

Closely related to the loricariids is the

Armoured catfish showing the six barbels and the spine on the pectorals.

family Astroblepidae, the members of which have lost their bony armour. The capitane *Astroblepus chotae* from the Andes has a sucker formed from the pelvic fins in addition to that formed by the mouth. These two suckers are used alternately to enable the fish to climb the vertical rock walls of waterfalls or potholes. Although progress is slow, the fish is able to live under conditions which would be impossible for other fishes. Since there are no predators to feed on it, the armour of the capitane has been lost.

The Doradidae, yet another family of armoured catfishes from South America, includes *Acanthodoras spinosissimus,* a slug-gish creature that spends most of the day buried in the sand with only its eyes visible. When removed from the water, the fish is reported to make a grunting noise but one that the author, as a boy, kept for three years, was almost dried out in that time with attempts to make it communicate, but never was a fish more silent.

In addition to their astonishing success in freshwater, there are two families of catfishes that are adapted to life in the sea. The Plotosidae contains *Plotosus anguillaris,* a colourful fish with longitudinal black stripes interspersed with thin bright yellow stripes set on a pale pinkish background. It is just as well

that this species is conspicuous since it is one of the most poisonous fishes of the entire Indo-Pacific area. Reaching 20 in (51 cm) in length, it has sharp dorsal and pectoral spines that can cause exceedingly painful wounds even from a slight scratch. A curious feature of this fish is a small bush-like process near to the vent which is joined to the vertebrae by a ligament. The function of this organ is not yet known. The second marine family is the Ariidae containing shoaling catfishes from tropical and subtropical seas. The females lay very large eggs, $\frac{3}{4}$ in (2 cm) in diameter, which are incubated in the mouth of the male for over a month, the fish being unable to eat during this period. These fishes are important in certain fisheries and the cleaned skulls are sold as religious and tourist curios under the name of *crucifixfish.

The family Malapteruridae from Africa only contains the Electric catfish a species which is described under Electric fishes.

If diversity is a mark of evolutionary success, then the catfishes can be considered a most successful group. Over 2,000 species are known, adapted to a vast range of ecological niches and displaying such curious habits as cave-dwelling and parasitism. ORDER: Siluriformes, CLASS: Pisces.

CATS, thought to have been first domesti-cated by the Egyptians, are today familiar members of most households throughout the world. Although various small cats have been tamed since prehistoric times the present-day short-haired domestic cat of Europe and many others parts of the world, which has been given the scientific name of *Felis catus,* seems to have been derived from the Cafer cat or Bush cat of Africa *F. lybica,* perhaps with some admixture from the European Wild cat *F. sylvestris.* Given the somewhat derogatory name of alley cat or gutter cat in the United States, it nevertheless makes up about 99% of the domesticated cat population of the world.

3

4

7

8

10

11

It is possible that most of the domesticated cats of India may have had a totally independent origin from those of Europe and that the Indian Desert cat *F. ornata* may have been its original parent stock. The common occurrence of spotted cats in India, comparatively rare in Europe, suggests their origin from this spotted wild cat. See also Wild cats.

A typical short-haired domestic cat is about 2½ ft (76 cm) long, including a 9 in (23 cm) long tail which, unlike that of the Wild cat, is held horizontally when walking. The weight varies considerably but up to 21 lb (9 kg) has been recorded. It is a graceful animal with a well-knit, powerful body and a rounded face with a broad, well-whiskered muzzle. The whiskers are used to feel the way in the dark. The cat uses its teeth to tear and chop meat. The legs are strong and well-boned, the feet small and neat with retractile claws which are kept in good condition by scratching on a post or rough surface. They are a great help in climbing and enable a cat to shin swiftly up a tree to avoid a dog, or to rob birds' nests or just to lie on a branch basking in the sun.

The colour of the coat varies considerably. The most common, the tabby, is of two kinds. The striped tabby has narrow vertical stripes on the body, similar to those of the Bush cat and European Wild cat. The blotched tabby is

The cat family includes species ranging widely in size, from those the size of a Domestic cat to the lion and tiger. Large and medium-sized cats are shown here: (left to right above) the lynx, puma, cheetah, jaguar, lion, ocelot, bobcat, tiger, Clouded leopard, leopard and Snow leopard, for which there are separate entries, as well as many small species, about the size of a Domestic cat, described under Wild cats.

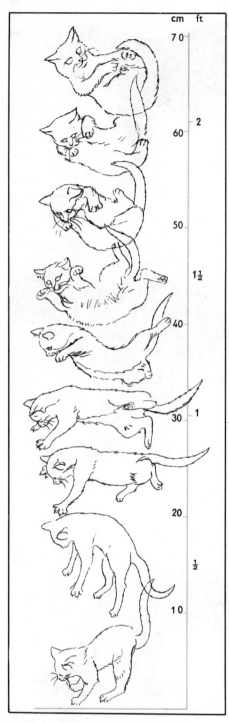

Dropped feet upwards from a height of about 2½ feet (70 cm), a cat can turn itself in mid-air and land on its feet.

arisen by mutation after the cat was domesticated. The pure white cat is either a total albino with pink eyes or a dominant white usually with blue eyes. Darwin was the first scientist to note that white cats with blue eyes are usually deaf. Subsequent research on kittens from deaf white parents has shown that although the ears of the kittens were normal for a few days after birth those of 75% soon degenerated to give deafness. Only a few of the remainder had normal hearing, some had hearing in one ear only.

There are many breeds of domestic cats, not all officially recognized in every country. American breeders in particular have been very enterprising in the production of new breeds and have introduced many new varieties. Some breeds are long-haired but most are short-haired. The long-haired Angora, said to come from Ankara in Turkey, and the smaller Persian, are now considered as one, owing to interbreeding. They have long silky fur with heavy ruffs of fur round the neck and thick tufts between the toes. The tail is long and bushy. The colour varies from pure white to grey. Some authorities claim they are descended from the manul or Pallas's cat found wild in Siberia, Tibet and Mongolia, but there is no direct evidence for this. The American Peke-faced Persian is a long haired breed which has developed superficial characters similar to those of the Pekingese dogs. Although grotesque in features it has nevertheless gained recognition and is popular in the United States.

Of the short-haired varieties, one of the most popular breeds today is the Siamese, said to have descended from the sacred, royal or temple cat of Thailand. It was introduced into England in 1884 and into the United States in 1894. The colour of the fur is remarkable in changing from pure white in the kitten to a pale fawn colour in the adult with the nose, mouth, ears, feet and tail dark brown. The eyes are a very bright blue and the tail is sometimes kinked. The forelimbs are relatively short and the hindquarters high. The related Burmese is seal brown with yellow or golden eyes and it lacks the dark points of the Siamese.

The Abyssinian is nearest in looks to the cats of Ancient Egypt. There seems no proof that it originated in Abyssinia. It has only recently been introduced into western Europe but is proving increasingly popular. It is a very lithe animal with large, yellow, hazel or green eyes but with a weak voice. Its coat is grey-brown to reddish. The Russian blue is also becoming popular. It has a soft seal-like coat, bright blue in colour and vivid green eyes.

One of the most familiar of the short-haired breeds is the Manx cat, remarkable for being tailless. It looks very like a lynx in outline and differs from the ordinary dom-

estic cat in its short back, its higher hindquarters and its habit of walking with a kind of bobbing gait. Although not a good climber it is by far the fastest on the ground of all domestic cats. In general its coat is double, with long top hairs and shorter hairs forming a dense undercoat. Although it takes its name from the Isle of Man, it probably originated in the Far East where many other cats have either very short tails or kinked tails.

A cat hunts by night by sound or sight and accordingly its hearing and sight are very acute. Its hearing extends beyond the range of the human ear into the higher frequencies and this is why a cat probably responds more readily to a woman's voice. It also probably enables it to hear rodents' voices when waiting beside a mousehole, when these are inaudible to the human ear.

Although a cat cannot see in total darkness its eyes are so constructed as to make the fullest use of any light available when out hunting at night. During the day its eyes are protected by an iris diaphragm which helps to exclude the bright rays of full daylight making the pupils become smaller until they are mere vertical slits. At night or in full shade of day, as in a room, the diaphragm opens fully, giving a rounded pupil to take advantage of all possible light. As with most nocturnal animals, the cat's eye has a layer of cells behind the retina called the tapetum, that causes the cat's eyes to glow, or shine in the dark, and to a lesser extent this can happen on a starlit night when there is no other illumination.

Domestic cats have departed less from their wild ancestors than dogs and have retained a greater independence. They differ also in their hunting methods. Dogs follow their prey mainly by scent and run it down while the cat, as has already been said, hunts by sound and sight, stalking with infinite patience and stealth or by lying in wait and finally pouncing on its prey. Nearly every farm has its farmyard cat that lives in the barn and catches the mice and rats and they are often kept in docks and on ships for the same reason. These cats are often semi-wild and mostly fend for themselves. Cats more readily go wild or feral than dogs and the number of feral cats throughout the world must be very high. Darwin tells how a few cats let loose in St Helena in order to destroy

nearly the same colour but has broad, mainly longitudinal dark lines and blotches on a light ground. In extreme cases the dark markings are relatively few, strongly drawn and standing out conspicuously against the lighter background. Such cats are recurrent mutants that parallel the King cheetah.

There are many colour varieties of the ordinary domestic cat including marmalade, ginger, tortoiseshell, blue, silver and black. All of the well-known colour variations have

There are many breeds of domestic cats. They vary enormously in colour though not in shape and each country has its own special breeds. Not all of these are officially recognized in every country. A limited number of them are shown on the next page: 1 Persian, 2 Marmalade variety of ordinary domestic cat, 3 Manx, 4 Persian, 5 Burmese, 6 Cyprus, 7 Siamese, 8 Chinchilla, 9 Russian blue, 10 Abyssinian.

The British blue cat, one of the many breeds of domestic cat which, despite differences in colour, are all much the same shape.

sacrifices offered to them. There are many pictures of cats in Egyptian antiquities and mummified cats have been found in tombs, especially in those around Bubastis, placed there during the 2,000 years before the birth of Christ. Many statuettes, figurines and amulets of cats have also been found. The tomb paintings of Thebes (1250 BC) show that cats were fully domesticated then. In two of these paintings cats are shown sitting under a chair and in one of these the cat is wearing a collar and gnawing a bone.

It was many years before the ancestry of the domesticated cat was fully investigated. The mummified cats should have enabled us to decide on their wild ancestors but unfortunately during the 19th century and early 20th century when a large number of mummified cats were excavated, they were used as manure on the land and large numbers shipped abroad as fertilizers. Only one skull was salvaged and sent to the British Museum. It was not until 1907 when Professor WM

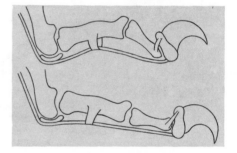

Diagram showing how the claws of cats (Felidae) can be retracted into their sheaths or extended, by relaxation of and tension in the tendon.

the rats and mice increased in numbers so as to become a perfect pest. He also tells how in some parts of South America the domesticated cats which had run wild developed into larger creatures of exceeding fierceness, inhabiting the rocky hills.

It is usually the larger cats which go off into the wild but there are many other unwanted cats that are simply taken out into the countryside by their owners and abandoned. There is some evidence that feral cats tend to grow larger than usual, possibly because of the availability of abundant natural food and because of a more athletic life. There is one apparently reliable record of a domestic cat going wild and doubling in size in four years. The maximum recorded length for a feral cat in Great Britain is 42 in (106·7 cm) overall but eye-witness reports suggest that a maximum length of 45 in (114·3 cm) may be attained with a weight of 30 lb (10·75 kg).

In breeding it is found that tabby is dominant over black and short hair is dominant over long hair. It is found, moreover, that feral cats not only achieve a size and ferocity uncommon in tame cats but that all revert to the tabby, whatever the colour of their forebears.

The cat's voice is the familiar 'miaow' usually indicating that it is hungry or wishes to be petted but it will purr with pleasure when contented. When angry or frightened, as by a dog, a cat will arch its back and hiss or spit. The long screaming cry at night, the 'yowling' or 'caterwauling', indicates that the male, or tom, is seeking to impress the female, usually called a she-cat when of the common or

garden breed, but a queen when she is a breeding female of pedigree stock.

Domestic cats are sexually mature at 10 months or less, the earliest record being $3\frac{1}{2}$ months. The height of the breeding season is from late December to March but the female may come on heat at intervals of 3–9 days from December to August. She is at her best for breeding purposes from 2–8 years. Males are at their highest potential from 3–8 years. Oestrus (heat) may last up to 21 days and is preceded by 2 or 3 days of excessive playfulness. Gestation is usually 65 days but may vary from 56–68 days. There may be up to eight kittens in a litter, but 13 are known. Very young mothers have only one or two and the number drops again as the female approaches 8 years of age.

Kittens are born blind, deaf and only lightly furred. The mother will often lift and move her young one by gently grasping its body in her mouth. The eyes open between 4–10 days. Milk teeth may appear at 4 days but it may be 5 weeks before all have come through. Permanent teeth are cut between 4 and 7 months. Weaning begins at 2 months.

It is generally accepted that the cat was first domesticated in Ancient Egypt or, if not, that the domestication reached a high peak there. In Egypt cats were the most respected of all animals as they helped to keep down the rats which attacked the grain stored in the granaries. The Egyptians even had a cat goddess called Bastet. Some people claim that 'Puss' is a corruption of 'Bast' but the more likely explanation is that the word is onomatopoeic, in imitation of the cat's hiss. Cats were kept in the temples in Egypt and

Flinders Petrie the distinguished Egyptologist presented a collection of skulls including those of 192 cats to the British Museum, that a proper study could be made. They were first examined by Oldfield Thomas who came to no firm conclusion about them and then they were put in store and not brought out again until 1952. They were then studied by Terence Morrison-Scott, who concluded that two species were represented. One was the Jungle cat *F. chaus,* the other a form of the African Bush cat *F. lybica.* From other evidence it seems that the Jungle cat, the larger of the two, was not domesticated but foraged around the human settlements. It was only occasionally mummified. The most frequently mummified was the Bush cat but, unlike its wild ancestors, judging from the pictures and statuettes, it was ginger-coloured with rather long ears and legs and with a long ringed tail.

Since the days of Ancient Egypt all sorts of superstitions or queer beliefs about cats have grown up. In parts of Asia it was believed that men became cats after death. The Chinese believed that cats could turn themselves into other creatures when they reached a certain age and both they and the Japanese thought that cats could talk when they reached 10 years old. In Europe black cats in particular were persecuted with revolting cruelty in the Middle Ages because of their supposed link with witches. The devil, too was often pictured as a black cat. Even today some people think it unlucky if a black cat crosses their path, but paradoxically most people now think of black cats as a sign of good luck. The saying that a cat has nine lives probably goes back to the days when cats were believed to have magical powers. It seems to have been the custom in the 17th or 18th century to immure the bodies of a cat and a rat in the wall of a new house to keep out the devil. FAMILY: Felidae, ORDER: Carnivora, CLASS: Mammalia.   M.B.

CAT'S PURRING, a familiar sound to everyone, but the mechanism of purring and its meaning are only just becoming under-

stood. Recent investigations by a French veterinary surgeon have shown that purring is produced by the vocal cords, the muscles of the larynx contracting rhythmically to produce a throbbing, resonant sound. Possibly the diaphragm acts as a resonator.

Cats usually purr with pleasure but they sometimes purr when sick or injured, although the purr is then harsher than the pleasure purr. Purring is also found in the Wild cat, ocelot, serval, lynx, and other small cats, as well as some viverrids. In the Wild cat, and in most of the other Felidae mentioned, purring is a juvenile trait, the kittens purring to the mother, and in the course of domestication this trait has been retained in the adult cat and is directed at humans, who are, in effect, 'super-mothers'.

CAT SHARKS, small and often colourful inshore sharks found chiefly in the Indo-Pacific region but with species in the temper-

ate and tropical parts of the Atlantic. The Cat sharks resemble the Carpet sharks in having the tail straight and not bent upwards, as in most sharks. They can be distinguished from them by the absence of fleshy barbels near the nostrils. There are two dorsal fins, without a spine in front of each, and one anal fin. The body is usually slender and graceful. A spiracle is present and, as in other sharks, this is correlated with the absence of a nictitating membrane or 'third eyelid' (see article on sharks). This family contains the species familiarly known as dogfishes, which are described elsewhere. It also includes the curious Swell sharks of the genus *Cephaloscyllium* found commonly in the Indo-Pacific region but absent from the Atlantic. These sharks swallow water or air when alarmed and are able to inflate their body to twice its normal diameter, presumably as a method of defence against predators (see also pufferfishes). When lifted from the water, a Swell shark will fill the

Pallas' cat *Felis manul*, of Central Asia and Kashmir. This Wild cat shows a similarity to domesticated cats.

Chartley bull, an ancient breed of Park cattle.

Highland x Hereford cow.

stomach with air and if thrown back will float until the air is released. Some of the Cat sharks are brightly coloured, for sharks, and the skaamoog *Holohalaelurus regani* of South Africa has a particularly striking pattern of markings on the body. Almost all the Cat sharks lay eggs which are contained in rectangular egg cases with a tendril at each corner. It is remarkable, however, that whereas *Galeus melastoma* lays eggs, the very similar and closely related *G. polli* is ovoviviparous, giving birth to live young. FAMILY: Scyliorhinidae, ORDER: Pleurotremata, CLASS: Chondichthyes.

CATTLE, DOMESTIC *Bos taurus,* large herbivorous mammals of the family Bovidae, exclusively living in some kind of association with man, their origins shrouded in archaeological confusion and conflicting opinions. Many domestic cattle will successfully interbreed with their wild relatives thus obscuring their lineage, and the picture is further complicated by the *Zebu cattle, which is described as a separate species with an independent ancestor, yet breeds well with ordinary cattle. Moreover, as man has migrated to settle in new lands, he has spread his domestic animals far and wide at different times and under a multitude of different conditions.

Despite all this, it seems fairly evident that modern cattle are descendents of the *aurochs, the wild bovid that once roamed

Europe and have become steadily more important with the continued development of human civilization. The first cattle were probably domesticated well over 6,000 years ago somewhere in western Asia and were later spread to Europe and elsewhere Even this is not certain, since it is possible that it was the idea of domestication, rather than the cattle themselves, which was brought to Europe. Several distinctly recognizable breeds of cattle had been developed by 2,500 BC.

The reasons for the original domestication of cattle form the basis of a longstanding and continuing controversy. The various theories advocate either religious or purely materialistic motives. In favour of the former, bulls have long been venerated for their great strength, and it may be that captive aurochsen were originally kept as a readily available supply of sacrificial animals. It is also suggested that the long curved horns of the aurochs represented an animal connection with the crescent of the moon, a favourite object of worship and a further reason for according special treatment to this animal. Certainly, bull-cults were very important in certain ancient civilizations, reaching a climax of complexity in Minoan Crete with bull sports (leaping and wrestling), sacrifices and the legend of Theseus and the Minotaur. Even today bullfighting and related sports are important social events in Spain and Southern France.

The more obvious reasons for domesticating cattle are concerned with the various products that these animals yield in the service of man. Cows produce milk and a copper relief from Mesopotamia dated at c.3,100 BC, depicts priests milking a cow. However, cattle must have been domesticated for a long time before they would have become docile enough to allow such intimate

interference without reacting violently. Cattle produce meat, another good reason for keeping them, and tame domestic animals near at hand would obviate the necessity of long and hazardous hunts for wild meat. Another suggestion is that in western Asia, the presumed ancestral home of domestic cattle, timber is, and was, in short supply. Cattle yield quantities of dung which could be used instead of wood as fuel and, far more important, their very large hides could be used for building huts, tents, shields and many other things for which wood was less suitable or not available. Yet another materialistic reason for keeping cattle is that they are big and strong and well suited to the role of traction engines. Sledges and ploughs, with yokes for attachment to cattle, have been found dating back to 3,000 BC, and the large horns of cattle would have provided very convenient direct attachment for ropes, long before the yoke was invented.

These ideas of cattle being domesticated as a source of milk, meat, building materials and power, are all attractively logical. There are, however, a number of objections, one being that many important cattle-keeping communities did not (and some still do not) kill or exploit them, but treat them with deepest respect and veneration.

Regardless of the theories, cattle are to-day exceedingly useful and probably the most important of all domestic species. They have become an integral part of Western civilization and have been transported with man to all parts of the world, even Antarctica.

Modern Western Cattle. These stand about 5 ft (1·5 m) high and weigh 1,000–2,200 lb (450–1,000 kg) or more, the bulls being heavier than the cows. They are grazing animals, nibbling grass with their lower incisor teeth biting against the hard pad of the upper lip.

Ankole or Watussi cattle, an African breed of the Asiatic humped cattle, or zebu, with enormous horns.

A herd of Asiatic cattle, called zebu or Humped cattle.

Cattle eat about 150 lb (70 kg) of grass in a day, at other times they rest and chew their cud (see ruminant).

Cows are mature when 18 months to three years old, depending on the breed and feeding. They are referred to as heifers before producing their first calf, and can continue breeding for over ten years. Usually only one calf is born, after a gestation of about nine months. Twins sometimes occur. Male calves are usually killed early and sold for veal; only a few of the best are kept for breeding.

Cattle products include fat, glue, fertilizers, soap and leather, but their main uses in western society are as sources of meat and milk. Cows normally produce milk only when their calf is small, but lactation is prolonged, in certain specially developed breeds, for several months. Milk production can also be extended by showing the cow its calf (a stuffed effigy is used by certain primitive herdsmen) and by the act of milking. Extended lactation allows the excess maternal efforts to be directed to the milk churn.

Breeds of Cattle. The great intermixing of different forms of cattle that has occurred during the process of domestication, together with considerable natural variation in the populations of ancestral aurochs, have resulted in modern cattle being genetically highly heterogeneous. Selective breeding, to encourage the emergence of certain desirable qualities, enables types of cattle to be almost 'tailor-made' for their particular habitat and purpose. Economically speaking, cattle are only machines for turning grass into money. In some areas cattle are needed that can produce good meat from poor, dry grass. In other places plenty of lush grass may be available and it is more profitable to keep dairy cows which yield large and regular supplies of valuable milk. Cattle are therefore selected as meat or dairy producers, with additional selective breeding to introduce features such as heat or drought tolerance, for use in tropical countries, from other breeds.

Purebred (pedigree) lines, bulls especially, are maintained effectively as genetic banks from which desirable features can be borrowed and introduced into crossbred varieties. Cattle breeding is a skilled business and the maintaining of quality of various lines is encouraged by cattle and dairy shows. However, extensive inbreeding tends to promote the manifestation of injurious features caused by the presence of recessive genes. These may become widely distributed as a result of using only a few bulls to produce many offspring. Nevertheless, the keeping of careful breeding records enables lineages to be traced (recessive genes may not become evident until after the passage of several generations), and gene carriers can be identified and eliminated. Genetic defects resulting from inbreeding can be financially disastrous, as in the case of an inherited tendency towards dwarfism in Herefords, and drastic measures are necessary to preserve high standards.

'Polled' is a term used to describe cattle which are without horns as a result of their genetic make-up, e.g. Aberdeen Angus. Polled varieties of many breeds exist, and an Angus bull will produce 100% hornless calves regardless of what type of cow it is mated with.

Britain is an important source of many basic breeds of cattle. Brief details of some of the more important and well known types are given below.

Notable meat producing breeds; Shorthorn. This originated in northeast England and is derived from a superior race of small horned cattle clearly distinct as early as the 16th century. It is a stocky breed with a level back and a deep body boldly marked in reddish brown and white; the horns are very short and sharply curved inwards. Modern bulls weigh up to 2,000 lb (1,000 kg); the cows are smaller. Shorthorns have a mild temperament and are therefore easily handled. They are popular as fine, sturdy beef-producing animals which will also give a good milk yield compared with other beef cattle.

Hereford. This breed originated in Herefordshire (western England) and was formerly much used as a draft animal. Herefords are very solidly built and their markings (redbrown body, white head and belly) are highly characteristic. They thrive on very poor grazing land and are reared strictly for beef production, especially where it is uneconomical to give supplementary quality feed to boost production.

Herefords are sturdy animals that withstand the rigours of heat, cold and drought very well. These abilities, combined with their utilization of rough fodder to produce desirable carcasses, make them ideal ranch animals. Consequently, they have been imported into more than 20 different countries as the basis for an important meat producing industry, notably in Argentina and the United States. Herefords are the familiar cattle seen being driven in great herds through innumerable cowboy films.

Aberdeen Angus. Angus cattle are short with a heavy build and straight back. They are black all over and hornless. They produce very high quality beef, well distributed on the carcass from a butcher's point of view. Angus cattle mature early and are therefore ready for sale sooner.

Notable breeds of Dairy Cattle. These are taller, more angular looking than beef cattle. They are bred specially for the quantity or quality of their milk.

Ayrshire. A large brown and white blotched animal, which is able to produce plenty of milk without needing the high quality fodder essential to the top dairy herds.

Friesian. Tall and robust (among the largest of western breeds) with variable markings, usually a pattern of black and white, which originated in the Netherlands. Friesians are famous for their generous milk production. They hold all the world records for sheer quantity of milk and butterfat. Many cows produce over 20,000 lb (9,000 kg) of milk (2,000 gall/9,000 lt) per year, and the record is 42,805 lb (19,262 kg) of milk (4,280 gall/19,454 lt), plus 1,246·4 lb (560·9 kg) of butterfat. The record production for a lifetime was an almost incredible 334,292 lb (150,431 kg) of milk plus 11,351 lb (5,108 kg) of butterfat. A good average yield is about 900 gall (4,100 lt) a year.

The milk of Friesians is very white owing to its relatively low fat content, a popular feature in view of the current healthy trend towards reducing the fat content of the human diet. Lower fat content also makes the milk more suitable for homogenization and sale in plastic cartons—important features in the modern world. Friesians have a docile temperament, essential in a cow that has to be

milked twice a day! Friesians also produce big calves which can be sold for veal. The cows can be used for beef when their milk production begins to decline. A drawback of the breed is that they do not mature nearly as fast as some other types of cattle.

Jersey. This breed was developed on the island of Jersey in the 18th century. Strict legislation prevented the importation of other breeds to the island, so as to keep the local stock pure and maintain their excellent dairy qualities. Jerseys are light brown or fawn with a dark head. They are kept on good pastureland as producers of high quality milk rather than large quantities. The milk is very fatty and Jersey cows thus hold the records for buttermilk production. Their milk appears a more creamy yellow than that of Friesians. Jerseys mature early and therefore calve at a younger age. They are also long-lived.

Guernsey. Fawn or brown and white cattle developed in the Channel Islands. They are hardy and adaptable and can be used for quality production under severe conditions. Commercial herds exist in the cold of northern Labrador and in the tropical environment of Puerto Rico; some have even been kept in the Antarctic! Guernsey cattle are mainly selected for their deep creamy yellow milk which has great public appeal.

In addition to these breeds, brief mention may be made of two other types of cattle. The Ankole variety are native to the shores of Lake Victoria and are famed for possessing the largest horns of any living mammal, up to 50 in (122·5 cm) long and 19 in (46·5 cm) in circumference. Chillingham cattle (=white Park cattle) are another well known type. Herds of Chillingham, Chartley and Vaynol are kept isolated in the British parks. They are of ancient origin, but were probably imported by the Romans and are not derived direct

from ancestral British aurochsen, as is sometimes claimed. The Chillingham herd has been fenced and isolated since the 13th century and so have been inbred for over 750 years. P.A.M.

CATTLE TICK *Boophilus annulatus,* a hard tick, typically found on cattle but also occurring on deer, horses, sheep, goats and other animals. It is one of five or six species normally restricted to the southern United States and Mexico in the western hemisphere, but it is also found in Africa and certain other parts of the world. It was the most important tick attacking livestock in the United States until it was eradicated by the United States Department of Agriculture.

There are four stages in the life-cycle, the egg, larva, nymph and adult. Once the larva attaches to a host it remains on the animal until adulthood. Only after the female completes feeding does she drop to the ground and seek a suitable place to lay her eggs. Ticks that have evolved this type of life-cycle are referred to as one-host ticks.

The Cattle tick and related species are responsible for the transmission ·of a protozoan disease commonly called Texas cattle fever, Red water or babesiosis, a severe disease of cattle in nearly every region of the world. See also ticks. FAMILY: Ixodidae, ORDER: Metastigmata, CLASS: Arachnida, PHYLUM: Arthropoda.

CAUDATA, tailed amphibians, also known as Urodela, have a long body with a long tail which is retained in the adult, not lost during metamorphosis as in frogs and toads. Their limbs are largely unmodified, the fore and hindlimbs being of similar proportions. They have a wide geographical distribution and are

The Palmate newt *Triturus helveticus,* tailed amphibian of the order Candata.

Western red-backed salamander *Plethodon vehiculum*, of North America, up to 12 cm long, ranges from British Columbia southwards to western Oregon.

found in most tropical, sub-tropical and temperate regions. They are, however, absent from southern South America, most of Africa, Australia and the Malay Archipelago. Linnaeus in 1758 recognized a single genus with three species. Today, 54 genera and around 300 species are recognized, usually grouped into four suborders, the Crypto-branchoidea, Sirenoidea, Salamandroidea and Ambystomatoidea.

The earliest known fossil caudate, from the Upper Jurassic of Wyoming (140 million years old), is the limb bone known as *Comonecturoides*. There is abundant fossil material from the Cretaceous (62–130 million years old), largely of Sirenidae, but it gives little direct information on the ancestry of the modern caudates.

Caudate amphibians range from 2–60 in (5.0–150.0 cm) and occupy a variety of habitats. They may be aquatic, semi-terrestrial, terrestrial or even arboreal. As in other amphibian groups the skin is kept moist by secretions from dermal glands. These glands pour secretions onto the surface of the skin, so preventing the animal drying out, a moist skin being necessary for breathing. Although many caudates have lungs the skin is important for the uptake of oxygen and the giving out of carbon dioxide. Some caudates lack lungs entirely and breathe through the skin only. In many species the dermal glands also produce noxious secretions as a protection against predators. In some species the hindlimbs are reduced in size or even lost altogether and the number of toes on the forelimb is frequently reduced from four to three.

The eyes are usually large and prominent but in some cave dwelling species they are very small and the animals are blind.

Breeding habits vary. Fully aquatic eggs may be laid or the eggs may be retained in the female and the young born as miniature adults. The young, or larvae, frequently have external gills used to extract oxygen from the water. These are generally lost in the adult, but in some species the larvae fail to develop into adults and retain their gills yet are able to breed. Such larvae are said to be neotenous.

Many of the caudates have the power to regenerate lost parts, such as a tail or a limb.

The classification is as follows:

Order	Caudata (= Urodela)	
Suborder	Cryptobranchoidea	
Family	Hynobiidae	Hynobiid salamanders
	Cryptobranchidae	Giant salamanders
Suborder	Sirenoidea	
Family	Sirenidae	siren
Suborder	Salamandroidea	
Family	Salamandridae	salamanders, newts
	Proteidae	olm, Mud puppy
	Amphiumidae	amphiuma
Suborder	Ambystomatoidea	
Family	Ambystomidae	axolotl
	Plethodontidae	Lungless salamanders

R.L.

CAVE FISHES, species adapted to a life in underground waters, usually caves but also artesian wells. Some 32 troglobiotic (cave-living) species are known, of which 18 belong to the large superorder Ostariophysi (carps, characins, catfishes, etc.), 11 being members of the order Siluriformes (catfishes). The remaining 14 belong to the families Syn-branchidae, Amblyopsidae, Brotulidae, Eleotridae and Gobiidae. In most of these families, the cave-living forms represent only a small proportion of known species, but in the family Amblyopsidae six out of the nine species are troglobiotic. In the Brotulidae, three freshwater cave species are most closely related to certain deep-water marine species, many of which are blind. It is noteworthy that cave fishes are found amongst the less highly evolved and not amongst the more advanced orders.

In most cave fishes there is at least some degeneration of the eyes, but in the extreme forms the eyes are no longer visible superficially. In the Mexican characin every gradation from 'eyed' to 'eyeless' forms is found, apparently depending on the degree to which the particular cave is isolated. Other features of cave fishes are reduction or loss of pigment on the body (which thus is pink or white), a rather small size (the largest, the Cuban brotulid *Stygicola dentatus* and the Kentucky blindfish *Amblyopsis spelaeus* reaching 6 and 8 in (15 and 20 cm) respectively), reduction or loss of scales (some come from scaleless families, however) and a tendency towards constant and active swimming. The sensory system of the lateral line is often, but not always, better developed than that in related surface-living forms, nor are the senses of taste, smell and hearing particularly acute. The basal metabolism, however, is much lower than in surface forms.

Cave fishes are concentrated mostly in the tropics: 21 in the New World, five in Africa and the remainder in the Middle East, Japan, India and Australia. No true cave fishes are found in Europe although partial cave forms (*Paraphoxinus* sp) are known which spend only a part of their adult lives below ground.

Most troglobiotic species are quite closely related to surface-living forms; the three brotulid species are an exception. It has been found, however, that the presumed stock from which the cave forms have evolved usually comprises species that already show some pre-adaptation to underground living. Such species are often reticent, preferring dark places, and have reduced eyes but well developed organs of taste and touch.

The evolution of cave fishes poses interesting problems, particularly that of eye loss. It has been suggested that since the eye in fishes develops relatively more quickly than any other part of the body, in an environment where poor growth results from scarcity of food it will be the eye that is most affected and will be most inhibited in its development. Other workers favour mutation as the agent leading to eye loss and it is thought this might be a positive advantage from the point of saving energy. See Blind fishes.

CAVE PAINTING, the graphic images, mainly of animals, which were drawn and painted on cave walls during the Upper Paleolithic era, and which are believed to be man's first attempts at pictorial representation. The distribution of caves containing examples of cave painting is centred on the Franco-Cantabrian region of southwest Europe.

The paintings were executed by means of a variety of techniques. Some images were simply engraved, others were painted in flat areas of colour, or in outline, using a form of paint which consisted of a greasy medium, probably animal fat, to which powdered clay was added. However, despite the numerous means by which they were achieved, and the varying quality of drawing, the examples of cave painting display an obvious homogeneity in terms of content. Cave painting is above all an animal art, and the representations of bison, ibexes, mammoths, horses, and like animals, occur over and over again. It is not likely that these were the only animals known to Paleolithic man, but they were the ones important to him, the ones that he hunted. He had no knowledge of agriculture or animal husbandry, and therefore he depended wholly on his ability to kill animals for meat and clothing. Seen in this light, any interpretation of cave painting as merely a decorative pastime seems improbable. It is much more likely to have

functioned as part of a system of rites and beliefs.

Paleolithic man must have perceived in the animals he hunted, a will opposed to his own, and in an attempt to ensure the success of his endeavours, he may have invoked imitative magic; a form of magic in which the belief was held that, by imitating an animal's characteristics, it was possible for man to gain power over that animal.   B.E.

CAVE SHRIMPS, a variety of crustaceans living in underground waters large enough to be seen with the naked eye. The term includes some true shrimps (order Decapoda), some Possum shrimps (order Mysidacea) and some amphipods or scuds, such as *Niphargus* (order Amphipoda). The latter are also known as Well shrimps from their occurrence in water brought up from deep wells.

All have parallel adaptations to their stygian mode of life. Most of them lack eyes, which would be of no use to them in the total darkness of the caves. In compensation for this the antennae are often much longer than those of related species living in surface waters. Cave shrimps are generally colourless. If brought above ground and kept well fed in the light they will often develop strong colours comparable with those of their surface dwelling relatives.

In many deep caves the temperature remains low throughout the year, and the

Cave painting of a wild horse on the wall of the Lascaux caves in the Dordogne, France, discovered in 1940. The painting dates from about 20,000 BC. Other animals portrayed on the walls of the caves are bison, reindeer and wild oxen.

Patagonian cavy *Dolichotis patagona,* the wild relative of the domesticated guinea pig.

cave-dwelling crustaceans have become adapted to breeding at low temperatures. If *Niphargus* is brought above ground and kept at normal temperatures it breeds during the winter, and stops breeding if the temperature rises above 65°F (18°C). In deep wells and caves, where the water is always cool, *Niphargus* will breed throughout the year.

Sometimes cave-dwelling crustaceans may be found in deep lakes whose depths sometimes communicate via deep channels with neighbouring systems of caves. A good example in Europe is the ancient Lake Ohrid in the south of Yugoslavia. This lake reaches a depth of 850 ft (286 m) and in the deep water lives a blind amphipod *Niphargus foreli,* which is known from caves in other parts of Europe.

The cave-dwelling Possum shrimps include *Troglomysis vjetrenicensis* from Herzegovina and *Spelaeomysis bottazzii* from Italy. Most of the true cave shrimps belong to the family Atyidae, which are also abundant in surface fresh waters. In addition there are a few cave-dwelling species of other families such as the Palaemonidae and the Hippolytidae. Among the true cave shrimps there is a high degree of endemicity. This means that a species is often confined (or endemic) to a single cave or system of caves. For instance, *Palaemonias ganteri* was first described in 1902 from Mammoth Cave in Kentucky, but has not been found elsewhere, although another species in the same genus, *P. alabamae,* was described from a cave in Alabama in 1961.

The best areas for cave shrimps are around the Mediterranean Sea and in the West Indies, but various species have also been recorded from Madagascar, India, Fiji and Western Australia. CLASS: Crustacea, PHYLUM: Arthropoda.   J.G.

CAVY, a South American rodent with no tail, short legs, small round ears and a large head, of the genus *Cavia,* which includes the domesticated Guinea pig. Wild cavies are represented by about 12 different species found throughout South America except in the extreme south. They range in size from a little smaller to almost twice as large as a Guinea pig, i.e. from about 8–14 in (20–35 cm) in length. They are fairly uniformly coloured in various shades of brown.

Cavies live in burrows in a variety of habitats but most commonly in open country on mountains, savannah and swamps. They are especially common along the chain of the Andes and avoid lowland rain-forest. They are sociable animals and the burrows usually occur in groups, rather like a rabbit warren. Strictly vegetarians they emerge at dusk to feed on grass and other fresh vegetation.

The gestation period of 63–71 days is unusually long for such a small animal, a characteristic shared, to a greater or lesser extent, with most of the hystricomorph group of rodents to which the cavy family belongs. The litter is small, usually two or three, and the young are very well developed and active at birth.

In the arid areas of northeastern Brazil is found a relative of the true cavies, the Rock cavy *Kerodon rupestris,* also a member of the family Caviidae. It differs from the true cavies in having longer legs and feet,

with nails instead of claws. Rock cavies are exceedingly agile, climbing rocky cliffs or trees with equal facility. In its way of life and in its physical structure the Rock cavy shows considerable convergence with the hyraxes of Africa although the latter are not rodents. FAMILY: Caviidae, ORDER: Rodentia, CLASS: Mammalia.   G.B.C.

CELLS, the basic element of organic structures; the units of life. The simplest animals and plants consist of one cell which leads an independent existence and displays all the major attributes of living organisms. The more familiar animals and plants readily visible to the naked eye are built from many millions of cells, each cell having some degree of structural and functional independence. An average cell might be $\frac{1}{1000}$ or $\frac{2}{1000}$ (25–50μm) in diameter, but different types of cells have very different shapes and dimensions. Thus the smallest cells known, those of *Mycoplasma* (resembling a diminutive bacterium), are spheres about 4 millionths of an inch (0·1μm) in diameter, an ostrich egg, which is technically a single cell, is about 6 in (17 cm) long, the cells of large protozoa may be $\frac{1}{10}$ in (2–3 mm) long and some nerve cells of large animals have processes which are threads several yards long. The larger cells and their main component structures may be seen in the living state with the light microscope, but the structure of smaller cells and the details of cell components can only be studied with the electron microscope. Much of our present understanding of cell structure comes from electron microscopy, in spite of the fact that this technique may only be used to study killed cells, normally after cells have been cut into extremely thin slices. It is less well known that parallel developments in other techniques have been equally important in providing complementary information about the functioning and biochemistry of cells.

Although cells are diverse in structure and in the components which they possess, they share many common features. The boundary of any cell is provided by a very thin membrane, about 3 or 4 ten millionths of an inch (7–10μm) thick, which controls the entry into, and exit from, the cell of chemical substances involved in the life of the cell. The membrane provides the barrier which permits a cell to function as an independent unit. Within the cell membrane is a solution (in water) of a variety of inorganic salts and organic compounds, known as the cytoplasm, which surrounds the other cell components.

The most important cell component is the nucleus which contains the chromosomes suspended in nucleoplasm, a solution rather similar to cytoplasm. The nuclear materials are enclosed in a double nuclear membrane perforated by large pores which permit the

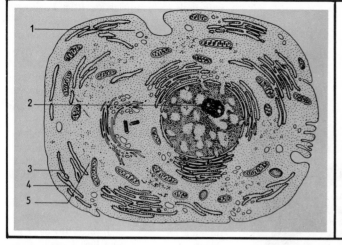

Using the electron microscope, which gives a far higher magnification than the ordinary light microscope, far more can be seen of the living cell than was imagined possible half a century ago. The diagram shows an idealized animal cell with its cytoplasm (1) surrounding the central nucleus (2) and embedded in it a variety of organelles, notably membranes (3) with ribosomes (4) on their surfaces and mitochondria (5).

passage of materials between cytoplasm and nucleoplasm. In bacteria and some other more primitive types of cell there is no nuclear membrane and the chromosome material lies free in the cytoplasm. In some specialized cells, e.g. the mature mammalian red blood cell, the nucleus has disappeared, although it is present and essential during the development of the cell. The nucleus is vital for the life of the cell because it determines the cell's synthetic activities. The information necessary for this synthesis is carried in the genes of the chromosomes.

Proteins form the most important class of substance synthesized in the cell, comprising complex and diverse molecules providing all the enzymes of the cell and much of the structural material. Certain proteins are characteristic of particular types of cell, e.g. haemoglobin in the red blood cell. The synthesis of proteins takes place in the cytoplasmic part of the cell by the assembly of molecular subunits, granules called ribosomes. These are most commonly found associated with the outer surface of the nuclear membrane or with the membranous network (endoplasmic reticulum) which ramifies through much of the cytoplasm. Materials synthesized within cells are often later secreted from the cell, e.g. as hormones or digestive enzymes. Such cell products are usually accumulated in membranous vacuoles which later move to the cell surface and discharge their contents.

The cytoplasm of most cells contains *mitochondria, membrane-bounded bodies the function of which is to provide energy for such cellular activities as movement or chemical synthesis by the controlled breakdown of large energy-rich molecules. Plant cells often contain in addition bodies called chloroplasts which have a rather similar construction, but contain chlorophyll and are responsible for the transduction of light energy to chemical energy in the process of photosynthesis.

The life of the cell demands a flow of materials through it. The cell of an animal needs a supply of food, and usually of oxygen, just as the whole animal does. Small molecules, like oxygen, pass through membranes almost unhindered, and there are special mechanisms for the transport of some larger molecules like glucose across the cell membrane. Very large molecules and food particles are taken into many cells, but since they cannot pass through membranes, they are taken into the cell by an infolding of a very flexible part of the surface membrane which forms a vacuole around the object and then migrates to the interior of the cell. Within the cytoplasm this food vacuole may coalesce with small enzyme vesicles called lysosomes, the contents of which digest the food substances within the vacuoles to liberate small molecules capable of passing through the vacuole membrane. Lysosomes may cause self-digestion on the death of the cell.

Membrane structures feature prominently in all cells, but the amounts of fibrous material in cells is very variable. Muscle cells, for example, contain enormous quantities of largely protein fibres that form the main part of the contractile machinery of the muscle. Many cells carry cilia, fibre-containing motile organelles which protrude from the cell surface, and a spindle-shaped bundle of fibres is associated with the division of the nucleus in animal cells. This nuclear spindle is formed between two pairs of short cylindrical bundles of fibres called centrioles, derivatives of which also give rise to the cilia.

New cells are only formed by the division of existing cells. The continuity of the information-content from parent cell to daughter cells is ensured by the exact duplication of the nuclear chromosomes before cell division, and their precise separation on the nuclear spindle at nuclear division to form two identical chromosome sets in the two daughter cells. Cell division is completed by the separation of such other components as mitochondria, centrioles and parts of the endoplasmic reticulum into two regions before the cell is pinched in two by constriction of the membrane.

While the cells of single-celled organisms, from the simplest bacterium to the most complex protozoan, are separate individuals which retain within their limiting membranes the ability to perform a full range of life processes, including reproduction, the cells of multicellular organisms have developed a considerable interdependence so that groups of cells become specialized for particular functions and tend to lose the ability to reproduce to form new cells. Thus, for example, red blood cells, muscle cells, nerve cells and cells of the salivary gland are highly specialized for functions respectively of oxygen transport, contraction, conduction of electrical impulses and enzyme secretion, but have lost other general attributes including the ability to divide, so that new cells for the performance of these functions can only be produced by the division of unspecialized replacement cells. In multicellular organisms the reproduction of the species is usually associated with the production of the sex cells, eggs and sperm, which themselves are very special types of cell, containing normally only one half of the chromosome number characteristic of their species—the normal number being restored when the cells join at fertilization. The sperm cell is little more than a nucleus, usually provided with a flagellum for motility, while the egg cell often has a very considerable food store as well as a complex organization, both of which are required for the early development of the embryo. M.A.S.

CELLS DISCOVERED. The cellular nature of tissues was discovered by an early microscopist, Robert Hooke, around 1660. A thin section of cork, seen under the microscope, reminded him of the cells or small rooms in a monastery. The cells that he could see were, in fact, only the cell walls, the protoplasm having died and disintegrated. Only plants have thick cell walls made of cellulose, for animal cells are bounded only by a thin membrane. They lack the regular, often rectangular, shape of plant cells and would never remind anyone of monks' cells. Nevertheless, the name has been transferred to animal cells, which is appropriate since they are the equivalent of plant cells.

CENTIPEDES, swift-moving invertebrate predators with a long, thin segmented body,

Head of a centipede showing jaws and antennae.

each segment bearing a single pair of legs. The first pair of legs are profoundly modified into a pair of robust pincer-like claws (hence Chilopoda—claw-footed) which meet each other horizontally beneath the head. The head carries a pair of thread-like antennae and three pairs of jaws, the mandibles and two pairs of maxillae.

The head consists of a single lentil-shaped capsule. The antennae are inserted on the forehead and the groups of simple eyes or ocelli, if present, are located behind the antennae on the front and to the side of the head capsule. One order, the Geophilomorpha, have a constant number of segments (14) in the antennae but never possess eyes; the other three orders have a variable number of antennal segments and usually possess eyes.

The floor of the head capsule is covered by the broad fused bases of the poison claws. Removal of these reveals the 2nd maxillae. Their removal reveals the 1st maxillae which are more modified and finally there are the mandibles lying almost hidden by the overhanging upper-lip or labrum.

The body is dorso-ventrally flattened. The *cuticle is like that of insects in that the shields or sclerites are strengthened and toughened by the tanning of the protein of the outer layers, giving them an amber colour in the absence of any other pigment. Each segment of the trunk is protected by dorsal and ventral sclerites with less armoured lateral or pleural regions between. Here the legs are attached and the spiracles open to the tracheal system (except in *Scutigera* where they are on the middle of the back). The hindermost pair or pairs of legs are usually held outward and upward as posterior 'antennae' rather like the anal cerci of some insects. The basal joints or coxae of these hindlimbs carry apertures or coxal pores, of unknown function. There are two genital segments between the last leg-bearing segment and the telson on which lies the opening of the single testis or ovary. A pair of accessory appendages flank the genital opening in the females.

A long tubular heart lies immediately beneath the dorsal body wall. The gut is a simple tube running the length of the body; a short anterior and posterior section is lined with cuticle dividing it into fore, mid, and hind sections. A pair of excretory Malpighian tubules run along most of the length of the gut and enter it at the junction of mid and hind portions. A pair of salivary glands open into the mouth secreting a fluid used for grooming the legs and other appendages.

The centipedes are divided into four orders. The Lithobiomorpha and Scutigeromorpha have 15 pairs of legs. The Scolopendromorpha have 21 or 23 pairs of legs and finally the Geophilomorpha have 35–177 pairs, the only order justifying the use of the term centipede. The number of pairs of legs is always odd—perhaps it is more useful to say that species differ by multiples of two pairs suggesting that there may have been some doubling during development.

The two orders with 15 pairs of legs are very similar in other respects. They have a common mode of development called anamorphosis; this means that the young hatch with fewer than the adult number of segments and further segments are added at each moult until the adult number is reached. There are further moults after this. The other pair of orders, the scolopendromorphs and the geophilomorphs, are also united by their mode of development which is called epimorphosis; the young hatch from the egg with the full complement of segments—quite the reverse of expectation since these two groups have so many segments. These two pairs of orders are often referred to as Anamorpha and Epimorpha respectively and each pair is further united by similarities of walking and breeding.

When walking, a wave of movement passes along the rows of legs, only one leg in eight

Centipede with young (Western Australia).

being on the ground at any time. The legs of one side are in opposite phase to those of the other, thus staggering the points of support. The centipede is pushed along rather like a boat with one oarsman with only one oar which he uses first on one side then on the next, the resulting course being rather sinuous. The fastest centipede is *Scutigera* which achieves a speed of 20 in (50 cm) per sec.

Geophilomorphs are exceptional in spending most of the time burrowing through the soil. Their sclerites are modified to allow movement by contraction and flattening of the body to be followed by a narrowing and elongation, rather as in the earthworm.

In all four orders of centipedes fertilization of the eggs is by means of indirect sperm transfer, without copulation. Males lay a blob of sperm on a specially constructed web and the female picks it up. In the two orders of

The Giant scolopendra *Scolopendra gigantea*, of Trinidad, reaches over 10 in (26 cm) and is ten times larger than most centipedes.

Anamorpha the eggs are laid one at a time, each covered with soil and, thus protected, abandoned by the parent, but in the two orders of Epimorpha there is further parental care. All the eggs are laid together and are protected by the female who periodically grooms them to keep invading fungi at bay.

Centipedes

She also grooms the newly hatched young for a short period.

Centipedes are mainly nocturnal, resting by day in leaf-litter, in the soil, under stones or loose bark and in crevices, and emerging at night to roam over the surface or climb trees and walls in search of their prey. Prey animals are immobilized by the injection of poison by the poison claws. The prey are usually invertebrates; the poison is not sufficient to immobilize even small vertebrates, nevertheless large species of *Scolopendra* do attack and feed on vertebrates which their poison only partially immobilizes. The poison can be painful and troublesome to man but never proves fatal in normal circumstances.

There are over 2,750 species of centipedes spread over all the world. Generally not much more than $1\frac{1}{3}-1\frac{1}{2}$ in (3–4 cm) long in temperate regions, they may be larger in the tropics. *Scolopendra gigantea* from Brazil reaches $10\frac{1}{2}$ in (26·5 cm) and the geophilomorph *Himantarium gabrielis* from Southern Europe reaches 8 in (20 cm). Most species are the natural amber colour of their tanned cuticle or deepened evenly or in variegated manner to brown, but large scolopendromorphs can be strikingly coloured, bright greens and blues contrasting with yellow. Presumably this is warning colouration. Some geophilomorphs can be luminescent and since geophilomorphs are without eyes this is presumably an unusual type of warning colouration. See *Geophilus,* House centipede, *Lithobius* and *Scolopendra.* CLASS: Chilopoda, PHYLUM: Arthropoda. J.G.B.

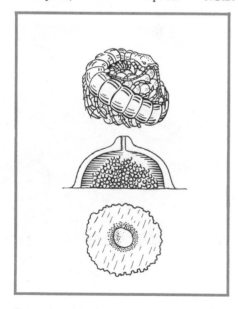

Parental care in centipedes. (above) Female coiled around an egg-mass. This is inside a 'turret' of earth, seen here in vertical section (centre) with a ventilation hole at the top. (Bottom) 'Turret' seen from above.

The cosmopolitan House centipede *Scutigera forceps* feeds on household insects in damp places in houses.

CENTROLENID FROGS, sometimes considered as a subfamily of the Tree frogs and like them have an additional element of cartilage in each finger and toe. They are distinguished from the Tree frogs, however, in having the end bone in each digit T-shaped and in having two of the long bones in the ankle region, the astragalus and calcaneum, fused into a single bone. There are thought to be about four genera, although very little is known about most of the species. They resemble the Tree frogs in their appearance and arboreal habits and are found from Mexico to Brazil.

Frogs of the genus *Cochranella* are green and about 1 in (2·5 cm) long. The skin of the underside lacks pigment and the bones and viscera can be seen through it. The head is broad and short and the eyes face forwards more than in most frogs. This gives them binocular vision which allows them to judge distances well, an important feature in an arboreal frog. Males of the genus *Centrolenella* have a bony, curved spike on the upper-arm which protrudes through the skin. Its function is completely unknown.

The breeding habits of this family are not well-known. The eggs are laid in disc-like masses on the undersides of leaves overhanging water and in some species the male has been reported to remain near the eggs. When the tadpoles hatch out they drop into the water where they continue their development. FAMILY: Hylidae, ORDER: Anura, CLASS: Amphibia.   M.E.D.

CEPHALASPIDS, primitive, extinct fishes belonging to the class Agnatha. Their nearest living relatives are the lampreys, but unlike them the cephalaspids had an extensive, bony exoskeleton consisting of a broad, flattened head-shield and thick, bony scales. The paired eyes were set close together on the upper surface of the head and between them lay the pineal organ and a single nasal opening; three depressions probably contained organs sensitive to vibrations. On the lower surface were a small, jawless mouth and ten pairs of gill openings. The trunk was roughly triangular in cross section. There were one or two dorsal fins and an asymmetrical, heterocercal tail. Paired fins were absent in some, but others had peculiar flaps attached to the head-shield.

Cephalaspids were not very large, about 6–24 in (15–60 cm) in length, and are thought to have been poor swimmers spending much of their time on the bottom where they fed by filtering the water. They are first recorded from the Upper Ordovician and seem to have died out before the end of the Devonian, a time-range of roughly 90 million years.

CEPHALIZATION, the process by which, during evolution, the head became morphologically distinguished from the rest of the

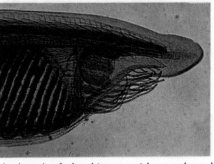
Head end of Amphioxus, with mouth and beginnings only of a brain.

body. This development can be correlated with taking up an active life particularly if the animal involved is long and worm-like. One end must lead and as much of the activity is connected with food finding, the mouth end leads. As the leading end is also the one making first contact with the environment, organs tend to collect there. Thus the head usually has the major sense organs on it. Such a collection of sensory structures evokes the development of concentrations of nervous tissue which will deal with the information contained in the sensory input and produce the motor impulses responsible for behaviour. Thus, cephalization leads to the development of a brain.

Sedentary animals, such as the coelenterates, retain a radial symmetry and the animals need to deal with stimuli coming from all directions. The ring of tentacles surrounding the mouth is the only evidence of a polarization of the body and there is nothing which could be called a brain. There is, however, a physiological gradient of dominance from tentacle end to base. Regeneration experiments confirm the existence of such a sphere of influence of the mouth-end and although the nervous systems of these animals are in the form of nerve nets distributed over the body, there is a tendency for some concentration of the tracts around the mouth. In Hydra this area appears to form a pacemaker for rhythmic activity in the rest of the nerve net, thus physiologically the onset of cephalization may be foreshadowed.

The free-living Platyhelminthes show the

Embryo mouse with large head and well-developed brain, which are proportionally larger than in the adult.

beginnings of cephalization, eyes and tentacles occurring at the end which normally leads in locomotion. While the nervous system remains rather diffuse some thickening can be seen in the head region.

Among the segmented animals cephalization has proceeded to a great extent by the fusion of a number of segments to form the complex distinguished as a head. One early stage in the process is shown by the polychaete worm *Nereis*. This animal swims actively, nearly always moving with its head forwards. It can, however, go backwards.

Another result of the fusion of segments which produces a head is that their appendages, which were originally for locomotion, may become adapted for collecting and chewing food. This tendency is seen in the arthropods where it is coupled with a greatly increased development of special sense organs on the head. Among Crustacea, for example, the antennules and antennae are brought into a forward position where they can most effectively carry out their sensory functions. They, like the eyes, are innervated from the cerebral ganglion. Beneath the gut and joined to the cerebral ganglion by commissures is the sub-oesophageal ganglion which supplies nerves to the mandibles, maxillules, maxillae and first and second maxillipeds. These appendages are found on the last three segments of the head and the first two of the thorax. All are concerned in the manipulation and mastication of the food while most of the remaining appendages continue to be used for locomotion and lose any sensory function.

The vertebrate head is the result of the fusion of segments, which are thought to have once been similar to those of the rest of the body. But the development of the jaws, the visceral arch skeleton and special sense organs have obliterated much of this appearance. Nevertheless, sufficient evidence exists to show that the head consists of a presegmental area followed by eight segments. The nerves of all these have been drawn into the brain and lie within the cranium and form the cranial nerves.   J.D.C.

CEPHALOPODS, one of the three largest classes of molluscs, it includes the squids, octopuses and cuttlefishes as well as a number of curious and interesting animals of types ancestral to, or derived from, these.

The Cephalopoda arose as a distinct group in early Paleozoic times. The early members of the class were all, so far as we know, shelled animals, like most other molluscs. They did, however, rapidly evolve a quite distinctive, chambered shell in which the animal laid down partitions behind it as it grew, sealing off the early parts of the shell from the last and largest cavity containing the main part of the body of the animal. The system seems from the beginning to have been associated with a capacity to adjust buoyancy by regulating the contents of the chambers left behind during the growth of the animal, replacing sea water by air (see buoyancy, cuttlefish and Pearly nautilus). With the achievement of neutral buoyancy, the cephalopods were free to evolve locomotor mechanisms quite unlike the creeping foot of the typical mollusc. The head and foot became modified to form a series of grasping tentacles and two folds from the underside of the body extended downwards to form a mobile, contractile funnel at the entrance to the final chamber of the shell. With this equipment the animal could scrabble its way along the bottom or swim from place to place, forcibly expelling water by means of the contractile funnel. The Pearly nautilus is a surviving representative of this stage of cephalopod evolution.

Further development of the possibilities inherent in these cephalopod modifications of the basic molluscan plan led to an explosive evolution of shelled forms, such as ammonites, in Upper Paleozoic and Mesozoic times. Many different species, some of them apparently very numerous, evolved and domi-

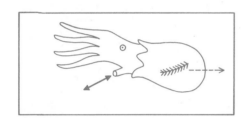

Top: *Alloteuthis subulata*. Portion of egg mass showing developing squids still with yolk sacs. Bottom: The young have just hatched.

nated the invertebrate fauna of the open sea; they included forms presumed to have been filter-feeders (the shell aperture is nearly closed in fully-grown individuals and it is difficult to imagine how they could have dealt with prey of any size) and a few species that were apparently sessile, a curious reversion to an alternative molluscan way of life.

Alongside those forms with coiled shells, a second type of cephalopod was evolving; a fast predatory animal typified by reduction of the shell in favour of streamlining and the development of the mantle cavity as an organ of jet-propulsion. In Jurassic times we find belemnites, the first distinctly squid-like cephalopods, in which the shell had become reduced and internal (though still, in part, chambered) and the mantle cavity, no longer surrounded by shell, developed as a muscular sac with locomotor as well as purely respiratory functions. These animals had arms furnished with hooks.

The consequences of this sort of development can be seen today in the squids many of which are sleek, elegant animals not, at first sight, at all the same sort of creature as the lumbering nautilus, now the sole surviving representative of the once vast array of shelled forms. Some of the squids have attained a considerable size and although nobody is quite sure how large, length measurements of 30 ft (9 m) or so are well authenticated and not uncommon. Even though the arms make up much of this length these are clearly very large animals by invertebrate, and indeed by vertebrate, standards. Reports of specimens twice as long are probably exaggerated, but it is hard to be certain since our knowledge of giant squids is

based on occasional strandings, and, curiously, on their beaks—the only hard part—found in the stomachs of Sperm whales. Neither sampling method would necessarily produce a realistic estimate of the largest specimens potentially available. At the other end of the scale are small streamlined animals, capable even of gliding flight, using the lateral fins as planes to sustain them in the air after a jet-propelled leap from the sea.

Evolved in parallel with the squids living cephalopods include a variety of animals, showing further possibilities of the cephalopod form and a range of degrees of shell reduction. The octopus has no shell at all. It has a series of shell-less relations that have secondarily returned to the pelagic life of their distant ancestors one of the most curious being the 'Paper nautilus'. The cuttlefish *Sepia* has retained the chambered shell but lives on the bottom, lying half-buried in the sand in wait for the small shrimps and other crustaceans that form its food. Like the squids it has two tentacles longer than the rest, and in *Sepia* these are kept folded away within the circle of arms around the mouth, to be shot out abruptly when the animal comes within range of its prey.

Alongside these active creatures are a series of deep-sea cephalopods that have become adapted to the comparative rarity of food at depth by cutting down on the rapid metabolism of their coastal or surface-living relatives. The cirroteuthid octopuses are flabby creatures, with a huge web joining the arms and a much reduced mantle cavity. They probably hang, medusalike, close to the bottom in deep water, hoping rather than hunting for prey. They are known only from specimens caught in deep-water trawls. The cranchid squids, and *Spirula* (a relative of the cuttlefish) hang or swim slowly about in the mid-water of the open oceans, isolated from the bustling life of the surface. *Spirula* retains an internal chambered shell. The cranchids, having lost it in the course of their evolution from more active squids, have developed an alternative buoyancy system based, surprisingly, on the retention of much of the waste products of their sluggish metabolism. Ammonium chloride, produced in the body, is marginally lighter than the sodium chloride in the sea and by enormously expanding the kidney sacs and storing ammonium chloride solution the animals are enabled to balance their own weight and drift quietly with a minimal expenditure of energy between meals.

Despite their range of forms and habits, the cephalopods are remarkably conservative in internal structure. They are still quite obviously molluscs: their gills are of the typical molluscan pattern as are their excretory, reproductive and digestive systems. Such differences as exist are clearly related to the accelerated pace at which the better-known

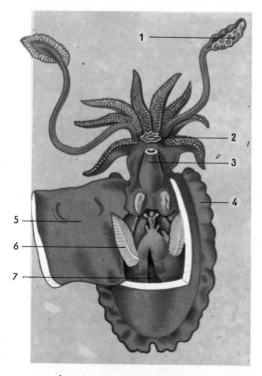

Anatomy of a cuttlefish. 1. sucker, 2. mouth, 3. siphon, 4. lateral fin, 5. wall of mantle cavity, 6. gill, 7. ink-sac. Top: cuttlefish swim backwards. Water is forcefully ejected from the mantle cavity through the narrow siphon.

Common octopus *Octopus vulgaris*, of European seas.

species live. They move faster, their muscular and blood systems, the latter with accessory hearts for the gills and a complete closed system of capillaries, being clearly adapted to a high metabolic turnover. The gut is modified for dealing quickly and efficiently with prey seized by the arms and chopped up by the beak. Squids, in particular, have broken away from the typical molluscan system of intracellular digestion in a massive 'hepatopancreas' towards extracellular digestion on a production-line basis. The nervous system and sense organs show considerable development associated with the need for rapid assessment and response inevitable in a swift-moving, predatory, but unarmoured animal and it is here, perhaps, that the

cephalopods have most distinguished themselves as something rather exceptional among invertebrates.

The surface and coastal-living cephalopods are predominantly visual animals. Like birds, they have to depend mainly on sight because they move too fast to rely on smell. The animals must, literally, keep an eye on the fishes and mammals that compete with them and prey on them in the sea. Their eyes are astonishingly like those of their vertebrate rivals. There is a retina, a lens with muscles for focusing, a cornea and an iris diaphragm. Laboratory experiments indicate that their visual acuity is as sharp as our own and that they can, in all probability, see colours much as we can.

In addition to this acute visual sense octopuses at least are known to have a delicate touch sense that enables them to distinguish not only the physical features of the world around them but also its taste. Using the suckers on its eight arms, an octopus can detect tastes (acid, bitter and so on) at concentrations far more dilute than the minimum detectable by the human tongue. From observations of the animals in the sea it is clear that this touch sense is very important in food-gathering as these animals feed largely on crabs, which hide in crevices where they cannot be seen.

Recognizing one's orientation in space is a problem common to all free-moving animals and particularly for those living in open water, away from visual or tactile landmarks. In the course of their long pelagic history cephalopods have evolved a system which, like their eyes, bears remarkable resemblance to the system evolved, quite independently, by the vertebrates. The cephalopod equivalent of the vertebrate labyrinth in the ear is a fluid-filled sac with internal flaps in three planes at right angles so that whichever way the animal turns, one or other of the flaps will be bent by the movement of the fluid in the sac. Nerve cells at the base of the flap detect the movement. In addition there is a calcareous 'macula', a gravity receptor hanging from a pad of sensory cilia.

Backing this array of sense organs, cephalopods have an elaborate nervous system, concentrated into a large brain between the eyes. Recent work on the nervous systems of the octopus and cuttlefish has shown that this brain is capable not only of very rapid assessment and response in familiar situations but also of learning by experience in the unfamiliar. These animals learn simple discriminations (differences between shapes and sizes, textures and tastes) as rapidly as many of the more advanced vertebrates.

Very little is known about the behaviour of most cephalopods. *Octopus vulgaris* and *Sepia* are well known as laboratory animals and there have been occasional studies of these, and of a few other species, in the sea. Octopuses appear always to be solitary animals, each individual selecting a 'home' cave in the rocks or a scooped-out hole under a boulder to which it returns between foraging expeditions in search of crabs and shellfishes.

There are often middens of discarded hard parts outside these homes, indicating that the inhabitant has remained there for a considerable period. The sexes are separate and, since the animals are not adverse to eating each other if opportunity offers, it is not surprising to find that signalling systems have evolved to indicate the sex of individuals when they meet. On the approach of other individuals of the same species male octopuses show a pattern of stripes (e.g. in *O. cyanea*), flush darkly and/or display the particularly large suckers that males have at the base of the arms (e.g. in *O. vulgaris*). Failure to respond with a similar display implies that the intruder is a female and copulation may follow. This itself is a strange process. The males produce sperm in packets (spermatophores) which are passed down a

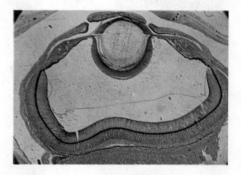
Cuttlefish eye: alone among invertebrates the cephalopods have an eye like that of vertebrates.

groove in the modified third right arm, the 'hectocotylus', inserted into the mantle cavity of the female. Mature females subsequently go 'home' and produce eggs, which they attach to the roof of their cave, remaining to guard them until they hatch.

At least some other species are known to make sexual displays and it is probable that these are general in cephalopods. Male cuttlefishes produce an impressive pattern of black and white 'zebra' stripes in the breeding season and the males of at least some squids (which, unlike *Sepia* and the octopuses live in shoals) have corresponding displays. Nothing whatever is known of the breeding habits of the open-water and deep-sea species, but at least some, for instance the Paper nautilus, show strong sexual dimorphism.

The eggs of cephalopods are large by molluscan standards. The embryos develop around a considerable volume of yolk and there is no free trochophore or veliger stage. On hatching the young of some species (cuttlefishes and some octopuses) are completely adult in general appearance and move at once to live in the sand or among the rocks on the bottom. Others, perhaps most, even among the bottom-living octopods, have a planktonic phase which serves to distribute the species.

The Common cuttlefish *Sepia officinalis*, and below *Illex coindeti*, a squid, both of European seas.

Cephalopods are good to eat and their fishery is of very considerable commercial importance in many parts of the world. See ammonites, belemnites, cuttlefish, octopus, Paper nautilus and squid. PHYLUM: Mollusca.
M.J.W.

CERATOPSIANS, a group of fossil reptiles belonging to the assemblage usually known as the dinosaurs. The ornithischian dinosaurs (order Ornithischia) are characterized by the possession of a pelvic girdle in which the pubic bone has an anterior prong. This type of pelvis is referred to as tetraradiate, to distinguish it from the triradiate type found in the other major dinosaur group, the order Saurischia, which lacks an anterior extension of the pubis.

The history of the ceratopsians is confined to the Upper Cretaceous and they were hence a thriving-group 100 million years ago. Ceratopsian fossils are mostly from North America, a small number have been found in Asia and it is possible that the group also extended into South America. Members of the suborder Ceratopsia have relatively large heads which usually bear large, bony horns. The skull is characterized by the presence of a large posterior bony 'frill' which extends over the neck region almost to the shoulders. This is an extension of two of the skull bones and in the more primitive ceratopsians it may have had large gaps or fenestrae, but in the more advanced forms it is quite solid. It was probably evolved to provide better accomodation for the muscles concerned in jaw movement, but it also provided protection for the vulnerable neck. The main variation in structure in the ceratopsians is in the size of the frill and also in the position and size of the horns. In *Triceratops,* of the Upper Cretaceous of North America, a pair of horns are present just behind the eyes (brow horns) and a single median horn is found on the snout (nasal horn). *Centrosaurus,* also from the Upper Cretaceous of North America, lacks the brow horns but has a large nasal horn.

The jaws of ceratopsians are usually drawn out into a 'beak-like' structure due to the development of an extra bone, the rostral, in the upper jaw. A similar extension, the predentary, is found in the lower jaw. The ceratopsians were quadrupedal and the hind-limbs were always longer than the forelimbs. The foot had four short toes each with a small hoof and the hand had five digits.

The more advanced ceratopsians like *Triceratops* and *Centrosaurus* were probably evolved from more primitive forms which resembled *Protoceratops.* Numerous specimens of this form are found in the Upper Cretaceous of Mongolia. *Protoceratops* has a neck frill, but this is widely fenestrated, and it does not have horns. SUBORDER: Ceratopsia, ORDER: Ornithischia, CLASS: Reptilia.   R.L.

Reconstruction of a scene in Cretaceous times a hundred million years ago showing a Ceratopsian.

CERE, the soft covering at the base of the upper mandible of the bill of parrots and birds of prey, including owls (from the Latin *Cera* meaning wax since it often has a waxy appearance). The cere is frequently swollen and/or distinctively coloured and in parrots it is often feathered. The openings of the nostrils are placed in or at the edge of the cere, and in some parrots are, therefore, hidden in the feathers. The cere is supplied with touch corpuscles and presumably plays a sensory role in dealing with food.

The apparently similar structure in pigeons—sometimes also called a cere—is the result of swelling of the operculum (nostril covering) and is not a true cere.

CERIANTHUS, one of a group of marine animals resembling Sea anemones, but having much more elongated bodies, up to 1 ft (30 cm) in length. They have two sets of tentacles, one set encircling the mouth, the other marginal on the edge of the disc. In contrast to the pairs of mesenteries in Sea anemones there is only one set of single mesenteries which join into the throat at the oral end. In contrast to other members of the Cnidaria, *Cerianthus* and its relatives possess an ectodermal muscle layer, so that the animal looks three-layered in cross-section. They live generally in warm seas in vertical cavities or burrows in the sand which are

lined with mucus and shed *nematocysts. Shed nematocysts and sand grains also adhere to the body wall giving the animals an iridescent appearance. See Sea anemone and Cnidaria.   SUBCLASS: Ceriantipatharia, CLASS: Anthozoa, PHYLUM: Cnidaria.

CETACEA, an order of mammals, including the whales, porpoises and dolphins, which have become specialized for an aquatic life. They spend their lives in the water and are helpless on land. Nevertheless, being mammals, they have to breathe air and carry out all the mammalian functions originally evolved for life on land, whilst living in a basically alien aquatic environment.

No fossils exist to link the Cetacea closely with other groups of mammals, the earliest fossils are already well defined whales. However, a number of features point to their being closest to the even-toed ungulates, the Artiodactyla. Their protein chemistry, the formation of the foetal placenta and the multiple stomach are surprisingly similar, but the gulf between the Cetacea and their nearest relatives is enormous in so many other aspects that it is probably wisest to consider them as the most specialized of any group of mammals and to classify them completely on their own.

The highly specialized form and function of the cetaceans is closely related to their aquatic way of life. The characteristic hairy mammalian skin has become smooth, so assisting streamlining. All that is left of the hair is some residual hairs on the snout and these are usually lost by birth or soon after, although they are retained in the adults of some species. These hairs have a sensory function in those adult species retaining them.

Cetacea have transverse tail flukes and swim with up and down strokes instead of the side-to-side movements of fish. This is more efficient for an animal which has to swim forward at speed and also to surface repeatedly to breathe. The vertical swimming strokes can be used directly, with only minor changes in body position, to control the vertical movements of surfacing and diving. Some dolphins and porpoises are comparable in speed with the fastest fish. Having a remarkable intelligence as well they hold a position of supremacy in the sea almost comparable with that of man on land.

The limbs still retain some evidence of the quadrupedal *pentadactyl pattern of vertebrate limbs. The forelimbs, modified to flippers, are specialized as hydroplanes, the basic bone structure remaining but active movement is virtually restricted to the shoulder girdle and joint. The number of digits (fingers) is reduced in some species but there is usually an increase in the number of phalanges (finger bones) of digits 2 and 3. Independent movement of the digits and phalanges is, however, lacking and the flexor and extensor muscles act as no more than braces of the bony structure and integument, producing firm yet intrinsically very elastic hydroplanes. The hindlimbs show as surface swellings only before birth. In most species all that remains of the hindlimb may be a single

bone anchoring the ventral body and tail musculature and the male external genitalia.

The neck is very short, the head flowing directly into the trunk. The cervical vertebrae may be combined to form a small single block or remain separate as a series of very thin discs. The tail acts as a lever on the resulting compact mass of head and trunk and hence practically all the animal's musculature is available directly or indirectly to drive the propulsive tail unit. Most species have a dorsal fin which acts as a stabilizer. In some species it is very large but in others it is small or even absent.

The nose or blow-hole is at the top of the head, allowing the animal to breathe or 'blow' immediately it breaks the surface of the water. The body, including eyes and ears, remain beneath the surface during breathing so that the whale's underwater life is unaffected. The blow-hole is equipped with an opening and closing mechanism and the underlying nasal passages have a series of valves and chambers. If water enters the blow-hole it is contained in the first chamber from which it can be blown on the next expiration.

Although not all Cetacea are fast swimmers, speeds of 25–30 knots have been quoted for some of the porpoises and dolphins. Even though this may be overgenerous there is no doubt that they can approach such speeds rapidly and for short distances. Some dolphins probably can maintain 20 knots for considerable periods, though normally swimming at 8–12 knots. Even if the body were perfectly streamlined it is difficult to see how such speeds are produced from the muscle available in a porpoise. It seems, however, that the skin has a remark-

able capacity for changing shape to automatically iron out pressure differences as the water flows over it and so prevent turbulence. Surface resistance to movement, or drag, is greatly reduced.

The order Cetacea is divided into three suborders:

Suborder		
Family	Mysticeti	– Whalebone whales
	Balaenidae	– Right whales
	Eschrichtidae	– Grey whales
	Balaenopteridae	– rorquals and Humpback whale
	Cetotheridae	– extinct
Suborder	Odonticeti	– Toothed whales
Family	Platanastidae	– River dolphins
	Delphinidae	– dolphins
	Stenidae	– Long-beaked dolphins
	Phocaenidae	– porpoises
	Ziphiidae	– Beaked whales and Bottlenosed whales
	Physeteridae	– Sperm whales
	Monodontidae	– narwhal and White whale
Suborder	Archaeoceti	– extinct

The basic difference between the two modern suborders lies in their feeding habits. The Toothed whales are, in most cases, equipped with simple conical teeth and feed mainly on fish and cephalopods, though one, the Killer whale *Orcinus orca,* also eats seals and porpoises. All the smaller cetaceans are Toothed whales. This includes the porpoises and dolphins plus some larger ones such as the Sperm whale *Physeter catodon* of up to 60 ft (20 m) in length. The Whalebone whales, on the other hand, although developing teeth in the foetus, lose them before birth. Instead they have complex comb-like structures, the baleen plates, which develop from the epithelium of the mucous membrane of the upper jaw. They include the longest whale, the Blue whale *Balaenoptera musculus* of up to 100 ft (over 30 m) in length, as well as other large forms, only two species being under 30

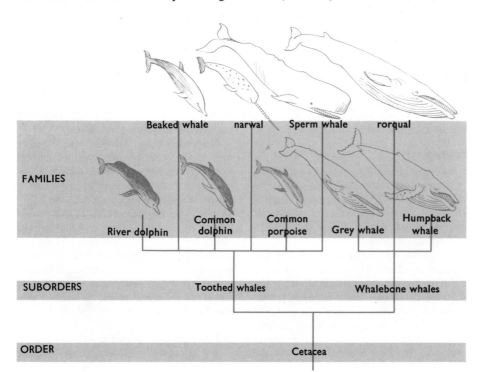

The order Cetacea includes the whales, dolphins and porpoises, which in practice are whales of different sizes. The order is divided into two suborders, the Toothed whales (Odonticeti) and the Whalebone whales (Mysticeti), the second of these being numerically the superior and showing the greater diversity.

The painting on the next page shows the difference between the Baleen or Whalebone whales (1–5) and the Toothed whales (6–12), as well as some fossil whales of which little is known. 1. Baleen plate of a Right whale and 2. of a rorqual, 3. arrangement of baleen plates in the mouth of a Right whale, 4. a Blue whale with 5. its skeleton, 6. a Sperm whale and 7. its skull, 8. Common dolphin, 9. Killer whale, 10. Common porpoise with 11. showing its air and food passages and 12. its skeleton, 13. the fossil whale *Zeuglodon* with 14. its skull and 15. its tooth.

ft (10 m). The baleen plates can be quite large being some 10 ft (3–4 m) in the Greenland right whale *Balaena mysticetus*. The baleen plates are used as a food filter. The whale feeds on small shrimp-like Crustacea, or krill, as it is known to whalers, which it takes in with water. The water is then pushed out through the baleen plates and the krill is left on the inside to be wiped off by the tongue and swallowed.

The patterns of feeding are reflected not only in the structure of the body but also in the behaviour. The large Whalebone whales are, in general, fairly slow moving. They are large and hence have few enemies, other than man and Killer whales, and speed is not essential for escape. Their food tends to be found in large masses through which they swim slowly, straining off food from water. In general the Toothed whales are faster, especially those that have to catch fast swimming food. Associated with speed in these forms is a high level of intelligence which makes some of them, at least, second only to man and ahead of the higher apes. Although no satisfactory studies have been made on the intelligence of Whalebone whales there is no evidence to suggest that it is as high as in the Toothed whales. But this concept may simply be due to our lack of knowledge of these large animals compared with that of the smaller dolphins which can be studied under proper experimental conditions in aquaria.

The intelligence of cetaceans is reflected in the brain size and in the high organization of the cortex. The brain of a large whale is, as befits its size, the largest of any mammal. The brain of a Sperm whale weighs some 20 lb (9 kg), but this is only about 0·03% of its body weight. On the other hand, a Bottlenosed

Bottlenosed dolphins performing in a seaquarium.

The Blue whale, largest animal of all time, compared with a man, cow, elephant and the extinct brontosaurus.

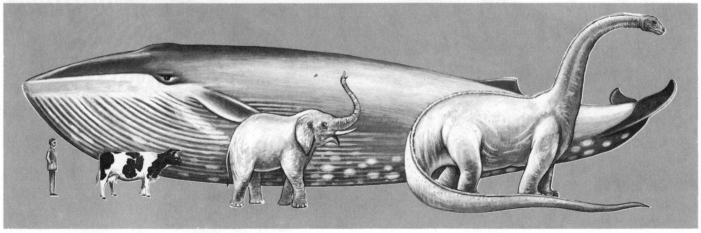

Studies in the birth of a calf to a Bottlenosed dolphin in Marine Studios, Florida.

dolphin *Tursiops truncatus* has a brain of something over 3 lb (1·3 kg) or about 1·2% of its body weight (compared with rather under 3 lb (1·3 kg) and about 1·95% in man). But weight ratio is not of great importance; a third of a large whale's weight may consist of blubber.

Although it is difficult to be precise about the functional significance of the various parts of the brain, much can be deduced from connections and analogy with other species. There is no doubt that cetacean brains are highly developed for fine muscular co-ordination as well as the sensory integration that muscular precision requires. The cerebellum, part of which plays an important role in fine muscle co-ordination, is highly developed, but the more primitive parts concerned with balance are less highly developed.

Cetacea have remarkable powers of hearing, reflected in the enormous development of the areas of the brain concerned with hearing. The remarkable acoustic development permits dolphins and probably all cetaceans to use a system of echo-location, sending out pulses of sound over a wide frequency range and receiving back reflections which they analyse. From the sound reflections they get much the same sort of information about the environment as a land mammal can get from vision under good lighting conditions. They can swim at speed through very complicated obstructions without touching even in total darkness in dirty water where vision is useless. They can also use their *echolocation to assess the consistency and size of structures, and the speed of moving objects such as fish. Hence it is hardly surprising that the motor co-ordination and acoustic parts of the brain are not only both highly developed but show considerable interrelationships.

The visual powers of cetaceans has long been a point of argument but in recent years, since the details of cetacean echolocation have become known, a more reasonable understanding of vision has become possible. Long distance vision under water is neither needed nor of practical value under most conditions; sonar provides the needed information. Underwater vision therefore need only be used for local reception. Above the water, however, some cetaceans, particularly the dolphins, show evidence of excellent vision. Some species on the other hand, particularly certain River dolphins, probably have poor vision. Information on visual acuity in Whalebone whales is scanty but unlike the dolphins the portions of the brain associated with vision and visual co-ordination is much less well developed.

Information on smell reception is lacking. It is often said that the Cetacea have no sense of smell but it is difficult to prove it and there is evidence just as acceptable to refute the view. Sensation from the skin is another nervous component which has been underrated in the past. There is also considerable evidence that skin sensation is more marked, in certain modalities at least, than was at first thought. The trigeminal nerve to the head region is enormous and there are some remarkable sensory end organs there. The skin around the blow-hole is very sensitive as also is the genital area. There is a great deal of sensory information arising from the forelimb. This is to be expected in a limb which, although acting essentially only as a hydroplane, needs to be very sensitive in order to control very fine swimming movements.

Respiration presents many problems for the Cetacea. They have the constant need to surface to breathe and also be able to dive efficiently for long periods. Many smaller species surface to breathe roughly once a minute and the larger ones rather less often. Even neglecting protracted dives, which some species perform, this represents a considerable respiratory efficiency. Although some 440 gall (2,000 lt) of air in the lungs of a large whale may seem enormous it is proportionally not much greater than in land mammals. In accordance with the need for quick air transfer, in under a second, when the animal surfaces, the trachea is very broad. The lungs are very long extending far down the body and it is suggested that 90% of the air in the

White whale or beluga *Delphinapterus leucas*.

lungs is changed each breath, far greater than in most land mammals. The bronchial tube is fitted with myo-elastic valves in dolphins and with a series of muscular sphincters in the larger whales. It has been suggested that when a cetacean dives deeply, air is pushed out of the alveoli into the bronchi, which prevents nitrogen from the air passing in quantity into the blood. This offers an explanation why they do not suffer from diving sickness which would occur if gas came out of solution in the blood as the mammal surfaces. Nevertheless the risk is not great, for human divers with breathing apparatus breathe air continuously at the pressure of the water at the level of the dive whereas the cetacean takes down with it no more than its lungs can hold. Probably also the obliquity of the diaphragm and the elastic chest wall limit the risk of 'squeeze', another danger for human free-divers who have relatively rigid chest walls.

The problem of storing oxygen for the duration of the dive is mainly solved by the large amount of haemoglobin in the muscles known as myohaemoglobin, which absorbs and holds oxygen. A whale has ten times more haemoglobin than land mammals. The muscles, also, are capable of working more efficiently without oxygen. In addition, a cetacean is less susceptible to poisoning from lactic acid and carbon dioxide, by-products of metabolism. And, finally, a whale's blood is redistributed during a dive so that mainly those parts of the body, such as the brain, which are susceptible to oxygen lack, receive a supply.

The heart shows no great difference from that of land mammals and the blood volume is not very different. One remarkable feature of the blood vessels of cetaceans are the retia-vascular plexuses (networks of very small blood-vessels) found in various parts of the body. These are of several types and have excited speculation as to their function in Cetacea. Most scientists have supposed they had some connection with diving but similar structures are also found in non-diving land mammals. Certainly in some situations they play a part in heat conservation, in conjunc-

tion with the thick protective and insulating blubber. In other situations they appear to play a part in equalization of pressure throughout the body in diving.

The stomach is one feature suggesting a linkage with the even-toed ungulates, in that it has three main compartments. The first stomach is essentially an oesophageal pouch which takes food into store before passing it into the main stomach where gastric juice, comparable to that of other mammals, is secreted. The third part is much smaller and varies considerably between species but digestive secretions continue here. Other than a considerable length, the remainder of the alimentary tract is undistinguished and it is difficult to tell where the small intestine changes to large.

The kidneys are remarkable in that they are broken into lobules, each of which acts as an individual kidney; a dolphin may have 400 and a larger whale as many as 3,000. The fewest are found in the freshwater dolphins and for this reason it has been suggested that the arrangement is associated with the problem of a marine salt-water existence. Although little is known about urine secretion in most species, those which eat invertebrates, such as the krill-eating Whalebone whales, would appear to have a salt excretion problem, due to the high salinity of their food. Fish, on the other hand, have a much higher water content and any species eating fish should have no more salt excreting problems than most land mammals.

Knowledge of cetacean reproduction is limited. Normal birth has only been witnessed in smaller species under aquarium conditions. Reproductive behaviour has also in general been observed only in the abnormal conditions of captivity.

The age of puberty has been debated and even in the Blue whale it has been put as low as three years but probably in the larger whales it is around five to six years and the smaller species a year or so less. The problems of fixing both puberty and longevity depend upon accurate ageing and although a considerable number of methods are available there are sometimes marked differences in results. Current views set the longevity of largest whales at about 30 years and porpoises around 15. The gestation period varies in a most odd way. Remarkably, the smaller the Whalebone whale the longer the gestation period: Blue whale nine months and perhaps even as low as eight months, Fin whale *Balaenoptera physalus* ten months and the smaller ones such as the humpback *Megaptera novaeangliae* about one year. The Toothed whales appear more logical with the smaller porpoises and dolphins having a gestation around one year and the larger rising to the Sperm whale at 16 months.

Most Cetacea have a set mating season but some species appear to be active throughout

the year. In some the season is related to seasonal migrations which allow optimal feeding and growth conditions for the new-born animals in warm water before moving into colder seas for feeding. Such is the state with most of the Whalebone whales. But many dolphins having no great migrations also have a set season.

In most species lactation lasts some six or more months the milk being of considerable strength with around 50% fat and 10–12% protein. This permits rapid feeding periods and also rapid growth of the young.

Little is known of reproductive behaviour outside the aquarium. Here, as would be expected with a highly intelligent animal, it is practised with considerable social activity; a wide variety of methods are practised to achieve sexual stimulation. Homosexual and interspecific mating is seen in addition to the normal heterosexual pattern. Whether such behaviour is typical of wild living animals is not known. But, as many species move in large schools with no fixed pairing structure it is likely that sexual behaviour is essentially promiscuous and social interrelationships essentially are free within the large group.

Birth of young brings social interplay between individuals; the mother moves out of the group, where she gives birth but with other females paying close attendance. These may even help the young animal to the surface to take its first breath.

Many cetaceans show a strong social sense, and need, such as injury or illness, brings others to the unfortunate animal's help. Such an animal will often be pushed to the surface of the water, periodically to breathe and this may be kept up for days until it recovers or dies. Even dead animals and especially stillborn calves may be treated in this way for long periods. Behaviour of this type does not necessarily represent a high intelligence though in many species this exists. Rather it points to a form of specialization where the need to breathe is associated with a conscious instead of an automatic effort. If the effort becomes difficult to achieve then the animal would be likely to drown without community help. Whether such behaviour occurs in the more solitary species, who in any case appear more able to lie on the surface in sleep, is as yet unknown.   K.M.B.

CHAETOPTERUS, one of the most interesting of marine worms. It is relatively large, often attaining a length of more than 4 in (10 cm), has an extremely varied body structure, an extraordinarily efficient feeding mechanism and is luminescent. *Chaetopterus*, in spite its size, is extremely fragile and if removed from the tube in which it lives, readily breaks. The whole body is translucent, apart from a few coloured marks on the head and the dark green pigment which fills the walls of its mid-gut and shows through the relatively transparent body wall. The worm lies completely within a tough parchment-like tube which it secretes. The tube is U-shaped, or nearly so, with each end constricted into a narrow opening. These openings may project as short chimneys above the sand. Tubes are found buried in clean sand, inextricably mixed with other organisms in seaweed holdfasts or on pier-pilings. They may be found occasionally near the low water mark of spring tides, but are more frequent below this, for if the openings of the tubes are exposed by the tide, the animal is trapped in a very small volume of water which it cannot renew and which must rapidly become devoid of oxygen and contaminated with waste. The narrow chimney-like constrictions near the openings not only imprison the worm, but prevent easy access by other animals. Nevertheless, other animals, which are tolerated by the worm, are often found within its tube. These 'commensals' include scaleworms and small crabs specialized for life in this habitat. They rob the worm of part of its food while gaining protection from it. Perhaps the

Chaetopterus benefits by their incidental cleaning of its tube, but the relationship seems to be one-sided.

As in other polychaetes the body is composed of a series of segments. In front, the prostomium is recognizable chiefly by the single pair of small tentacles or antennae. The anterior ten pairs of parapodia are similar and fairly short, the 11th pair extends as long arms from which mucus is secreted for feeding. Immediately behind these arms is an elongated segment with a ciliated groove mid-dorsally ending in a prominent cup. The groove extends forwards between the arms, which represent the dorsal or notopodial lobes of that segment, as far as the head. Behind the ciliated cup there are three prominent fans.

The animal feeds by straining the water pumped through its tube by the fans which beat to and fro like balers. A fully-grown worm can pump over 2 pt (1 lt) an hour through its tube. A thin mucous sheet is secreted by the notopodial arms which are held outstretched against the sides of the tube

so that all the water pumped has to pass through it. Particles as small as 40 Å (4 millionths of a mm) can be retained. All micro-organisms, and even some large protein molecules, will be caught on the mucous sheet. From time to time this becomes loaded and is then rolled up into a ball in the dorsal ciliated cup and passed forward along the ciliated groove to the head. It is passed into the mouth with the help of the tentacles. The whole process is repeated with clockwork regularity.

If a *Chaetopterus* is removed from its tube and swirled round in a bowl of sea water in a darkened room, it will be seen to luminesce vividly. Three or four worms together can produce enough light, at least for a few moments, by which to read a newspaper. The light is produced by a luminous substance secreted into the water by special glands. It is not obvious what use this is to the animal, for in nature it never leaves its tube. FAMILY: Chaetopteridae, CLASS: Polychaeta, PHYLUM: Annelida.   R.P.D.

CHAFERS, a large group of beetles related to the Dor beetles and Dung beetles and distributed throughout the world. In Europe, the Garden chafer or June bug *Phyllopertha horticola*, $\frac{2}{5}$ in (4 mm) long, has a green head and thorax and a dark yellowish red abdomen while the Common European chafer or cockchafer *Melolontha melolontha*, 1 in (2·5 cm) long, is a large reddish-brown beetle often occurring in huge swarms around trees in early summer. In North America, other chafers, especially noticed because they bang into lighted windows or car windscreens, are called May bugs or June bugs. In Assam, the Giant cockchafer reaches a length of 3 in (7·6 cm) with front legs of over $2\frac{1}{2}$ in (6·3 cm), each bearing two sharp spurs.

Both larval and adult chafers damage plants. The larvae, large white C-shaped grubs, live in the soil or in rotting wood and do much damage to the roots or plants while the adults eat the leaves and petals or suck sap and nectar. FAMILY: Scarabaeidae, ORDER: Coleoptera, CLASS: Insecta, PHYLUM: Arthropoda.

CHAFFINCH, certain birds of the finch family Fringillidae, subfamily Fringillinae; principally the chaffinch, *Fringilla coelebs*, common in Europe. The Canary Islands chaffinch, *F. teydea* is also known simply as chaffinch. See also finch. FAMILY: Fringillidae, ORDER: Passeriformes, CLASS: Aves.

CHALCID WASPS, sometimes called Chalcid flies, a family which includes some of the smallest of all insects with bodies only 0·25 mm in length. Chalcids can be distinguished immediately from typical wasps, for their body has no 'waist' between the thorax and abdomen. Another distinguishing

A small school of Bottlenosed whales *Hyperoodon rostratus* surfacing at sea.

character of the chalcids can be found in the structure of the hindlegs, in which the femur is greatly enlarged and, as a rule, very conspicuous. Many chalcids lay their eggs in the eggs of other insects and when the larval wasp hatches it eats the tissues of its host. In this way, these wasps can inflict heavy mortality on the populations of insects injurious to Man, and are used in the biological control of pests. FAMILY: Chalcididae, ORDER: Hymenoptera, CLASS: Insecta, PHYLUM: Arthropoda.

CHALICOTHERES, a group of fossil mammals which ranged in time from the Eocene to the Pleistocene. The earliest forms are found in North America and Asia, the latest in Asia

and Africa, but some are found in Europe.

Cuvier, the 19th century French zoologist, maintained that, because all the parts of an animal were functional components of one system, it would be possible to reconstruct any animal from a single one of its bones. When the skull and teeth of chalicotheres were first discovered, they were correctly recognized as being very like those of early horses and their allies, and were classified as perissodactyls. In fact, Cuvier had already described part of chalicothere skeleton as belonging to a pangolin for, surprisingly, the chalicotheres had claws! How they lived is something of a mystery. One obvious suggestion is that the claws were used for digging up roots, but the teeth show no signs of the heavy

wear this would occasion. More probably, they used to browse on trees, using the claws as hooks to pull branches down to the mouth. FAMILY: Chalicotheridae, ORDER: Perissodactyla, CLASS: Mammalia.

CHAMELEONS, old world lizards especially noted for their adaptation to life in the branches of trees and shrubs. There are two genera with 90 species in the family; the genus *Chamaeleo* is by far the biggest with about 70 species. Some authors distribute the 20 species of the Stump-tailed chameleon amongst various genera, but here they are considered to belong to genus *Brookesia*. Most chameleon species are to be found in tropical Africa and Madagascar. Although the variety of species lessens southwards chameleons can also be found in the Cape Province in southern Africa. The Common chameleon *Chamaeleo chamaeleon* is the most northern representative of the family and can be found in North Africa, southern Spain and Portugal, Malta, Krete in the north of the Arabian peninsula and in India and Ceylon. Most chameleons are medium sized lizards of about 6–12 in (15–30 cm) length, but there are some tiny ones of just a few centimetres in length (e.g. species of the genus *Brookesia*) and some giants amongst the species of the genus *Chamaeleo* that reportedly reached a length of 32 in (80 cm) in some forms in Madagascar and Africa.

The chameleon's body is usually flattened from side to side; the head often has a showy crest, horns or skinfolds. The teeth are acrodont like those of the agamas. The eyelids are grown over to a circle of about the size of a pupil out of which the big eyeballs protrude on each side of the head. The eyes can be moved independently of each other which especially fascinates the human contemplator. The chameleon's tongue is not slit like that of most lizards. Instead it is built like a catapult with a club-like tip and can be shot out at high speed to a length greater than the chameleon's total body length. The prey is hit by the tip of the tongue, glued to it and drawn back to the mouth at the same speed. The shooting out of the tongue greatly increases the radius within which food can be caught. The size of the prey depends on the size of the chameleon itself: small to medium-sized ones will catch mainly insects; the large ones will also capture other lizards, small mammals and birds.

The tongue bone is well developed in all chameleons and plays an important part in

Like lightning the tongue of the chameleon (*Chamaeleo*) shoots outwards. The prey is caught by the split tip of the tongue, not by a sticky slime on the tongue, as was formerly thought.

The common chameleon of the southern half of Africa is *Chamaeleo dilepis* (opposite).

the catapult mechanism of the tongue. While at rest the muscular tongue is curled around the tongue bone. Before shooting the circular muscles at the back end of the tongue contract violently and try to push the tongue down from the pointed continuation of the tongue bone. This, however, is only possible after the longitudinal muscles relax and thus become inefficient in their role as adversaries to the circular muscles. As this relaxation is very sudden the tongue shoots out of the mouth under the resulting pressure, rather as one would shoot an orange pip by squeezing it with the finger-tips. It is withdrawn together with the glued-on prey through the elasticity of the tissue and a repeated contraction of the longitudinal muscles.

The limbs of a chameleon are long, thin

Female chameleon *Chamaeleo pardalis.*

An unusually marked chameleon.

and carry the body rather high. The toes are united into two opposing bundles on each foot: two toes on the outside and three on the inside on the front feet and three on the outside and two on the inside on the hind feet. This has changed each foot into a pair of clasping tongs that enable the chameleon to get a firm grip on a perch. In addition the species of the genus *Chamaeleo* have a prehensile tail which even on its own could support the weight of the body.

The chameleon's ability to change its colour is well known although the layman often has a greatly exaggerated idea of this.

Male of *Chamaeleo jacksoni* showing three horns. Other species may have one to five horns.

The physiological colour change in most chameleons is, however, a very noticeable and quick process. But the chameleon cannot always match its surroundings. The body colouration of the day-active arboreal chameleons is a good protection, for example, a green or bark-coloured skin according to environment. Very often, however, colouration and markings play a part in disputes with another member of the same species; sometimes they just mirror a specific physiological condition. A surprising number of chameleons have a pale whitish sleeping colouration and with the help of a torch can easily be found in the dark foliage where they would be completely protected by their colour during the day. Male and sometimes also female chameleons hold territories which they will defend jealously against others. But only very rarely do real fights take place although the horns and crests on the heads of a number of species would probably make good weapons. When the two rivals are at viewing distance they threaten each other by displaying their brilliant colours, always showing the side of the inflated body to the enemy in order to look

more impressive. Characteristic swayings of the body emphasize the threat posture and sometimes the mouth is opened wide to show the contrasting colouration of the mucous membrane.

In the wild this psychological warfare is usually sufficient to force an opponent to retreat. Only under the restricted conditions in captivity do real fights occur and the bites can inflict serious wounds and sometimes even kill a rival. The defeated male will assume the unobtrusive colours of either a female or young one and retreat slowly. The victor will let him go without further interference: through the change in colour he has become uninteresting and is no longer a rival.

Because of their bizarre appearance and their interesting biology chameleons are favourites in terrariums. But the results of captivity are not very encouraging. Usually they die after a few months even if they took food initially. Only occasionally can specimens of a few species be kept and bred in a terrarium. One of the many reasons for this failure is the strict holding of territories which makes it impossible to keep one male within range of sight of another of the same species.

Most chameleons lay eggs which the female deposits in holes in the ground which she has previously dug herself. Digging holes into the ground and laying eggs in them is a highly dangerous affair for the arboreal chameleon. Some species, mainly in the subtropical climate of southern Africa and in some higher parts of the highlands have become viviparous. The fully developed young ones are born in their egg membrane; they free themselves of this membrane immediately after birth and start an individual life. They need no guidance from their parents to become expert hunters. FAMILY: Chamaeleonidae, ORDER: Squamata, CLASS: Reptilia.   K.K.

CHAMOIS *Rupicapra rupicapra,* one of the so-called 'goat-antelopes', mountain-living and closely related to the goats; famous for its agility. 30–32 in (75–80 cm) high, both sexes are of approximately equal size. Most individuals weigh 77–100 lb (35–45 kg), but members of the largest race, from the Carpathians, may weigh as much as 130 lb (60 kg). Chamois have stiff coarse hair, fawn or brown in summer and dark, nearly black, in winter; there is a black dorsal stripe and flank-band and the legs are black; the underparts are white and so is the face, except for a thick black line from the base of the horns through the eye to the muzzle (the gazelle face-pattern). The hoof pad is somewhat

elastic, giving the animal an enviable surefootedness. The horns are upright, thin and hooked back at the tip.

Chamois are found on all the major mountain-ranges of Europe and Asia Minor: the Pyrenees, Cantabrian range, Chartreuse massif, Alps, Apennines, Tyrol, Tatra, Carpathians, Balkans, Pindus, Taurus and the Caucasus. Slightly different races are found on each range. They live in herds of 15–30, consisting of females and young; the males are solitary for most of the year, some being attached to the herds, following slowly behind as the herd moves along, single file. In the rutting season, August to October, big bisexual herds are formed and the actual rut takes place at the end of October and beginning of November, when the males fight for possession of harems. Some harems are possessed by up to three males; most by only one. The male has glands behind the horns, which enlarge in the rutting season. The big herds reform after the rut, breaking up again into the summer separate-sex pattern at the end of winter. Gestation is anything from 153 to 210 days. In the Caucasus the young, usually single but sometimes two or three, are born in early or mid-May; in the Alps, one month later. Females mature at two years, males at three to four. A chamois may live as long as 22 years.

Chamois generally inhabit the alpine zone, between the forests and the snowline; they have been recorded as high · as 15,430 ft

(4,750 m) on Mt Blanc. In winter they descend to feed on pine shoots and moss in the forest. Each herd has a sentinel, which whistles and stamps when alarmed. FAMILY: Bovidae, ORDER: Artiodactyla, CLASS: Mammalia.   C.P.G.

CHARACINS or tetras, small fairly primitive, freshwater fishes. The term characin is not easy to define because of its frequent use and loose application in non-scientific literature. Not all members of the family Characidae are termed characins while the names characin and tetra are used, sometimes interchangeably, for members of other families. The name characin is here used for the members of the family Characidae, while the wider term characoid is used for all members of the 16 families making up the suborder Characoidei.

The characoid fishes typically have well developed jaw teeth, a non-protrusile mouth, a single dorsal and anal fin and usually an adipose fin. They are allied to the carp-like fishes (suborder Cyprinoidei), but the latter lack teeth in the jaws, have a protrusile mouth and no adipose fin. The characoids are found in South America and in Africa and this distribution has been taken as evidence that the two continents were once joined but later drifted apart (see Continental drift theory). The carp-like fishes are believed to have evolved from the characoid line but the two groups occur together only in Africa.

Apart from their leaping powers chamois are noted for their keen sight and hearing, making them difficult to stalk.

Since the carp-like fishes invaded Africa from the east, that is from Asia, and are absent from South America, the separation of Africa and America must have occurred before the carp-like fishes arrived. Characoid fishes are present in the southern part of the United States, but this is evidently a fairly recent invasion since the bridge between the two continents has not long existed, geologically speaking.

The family Characidae contains about 1,500 species in South and Central America, as well as some genera in Africa. Most of the characins are carnivorous and all are egg-layers. In South America they include fishes of many different shapes and habits. There are small shoaling species, large predatory species, pike-like species, deep-bodied bream-like species, highly coloured species and species which are almost transparent. Some of the characins have a superficial resemblance to highly specialized fishes from other groups. *Ichthyoelephas,* for example, resembles the catastomid suckers of North America, while *Luciocharax* resembles the North American garpikes. The characins, like the carp-like fishes, have shown considerable flexibility in their evolution, a basic body plan having become adapted to many different modes of life.

The voracious pirhanas, which are described elsewhere, are not the only savage carnivores amongst the characins. In Africa the tigerfishes are equally voracious and grow to a much larger size, *Hydrocynus goliath* weighing up to 130 lb (59 kg) and well justifying its specific name. It is a favourite sporting fish and can prove dangerous when being landed. The genus *Hoplias* from central parts of South America is also known as the tigerfish. It is a thick-set, primitive form that has sharp teeth, lacks an adipose fin and grows to 18 in (50 cm). The rather similar *Erythrinus* is of interest because the swimbladder has been modified

South American Jewel tetra *Hyphessobrycon callistus.*

into an accessory air-breathing organ. It also lacks an adipose fin.

Members of the genus *Mylossoma* (and also *Myloplus* and *Metynnis*) are deep-bodied forms with much the same elegant shape as the pirhana but without its voracious habits. They can be safely introduced into an aquarium. *Myloplus arnoldi* has a silvery body with a delicate yellow tinge, the dorsal, adipose and tail fins being orange with a black border and the anal fin, which is produced into a sickle-shape in front, is a deep orange to blood-red in colour. *Metynnis maculatus,* another pretty South American characin imported into Europe, has dark brown spots on a muddy background, a shining orange spot on the gill cover followed by a darker spot, and a brick-red to orange anal fin and tail with dark edges. Members of the genus *Moenkhausia* are commonly kept in aquaria and are attractive deep-bodied forms with long anal fins and often with shining scales. Similar, but with an exaggeration of the shape are the Black widows.

The penguinfish *Thayeria obliqua* from the Amazon has a compressed, elongated body and is olive green with a black stripe

running through to the lower lobe of the tail. When the fish is in good condition there is a golden lower edge to the stripe. These fishes seem to rest in muddy water with their heads held up.

The bloodfin *Aphyocharax rubripinnis* from Argentina can stand lower temperatures than the species from the Amazon. It is a small and slim fish with a silver-grey body and bright red fins.

The X-ray fish *Pristella riddlei* grows to about 2 in (5 cm) and is found in much of the northern part of South America. Its common name stems from its almost transparent body, the bones being visible as well as the blood vessels, although the intestines are hidden by the silvery body wall. The dorsal fin has a black spot near its tip and is fringed with white. The fish provides an excellent lesson in living anatomy.

One of the most widespread of tropical American genera is *Astynax,* found from Arizona to Patagonia. Members of *Astynax* live in a wide range of habitats, from lakes to caves and from mountain streams to estuaries. These fishes have moderately deep, compressed bodies, tapering from behind the pelvic fins to the tail. Most of the species are placid and unspectacular, but two deserve mention. *Astynax fasciatus* is typical of the genus and lives in streams in Mexico. In the same region, but living in subterranean pools and streams near San Luis Potosi is the blind cave characin *Astynax jordani.* It is almost identical to *A. fasciatus* in general shape but the eyes are minute and covered in skin so that the fish cannot see. In colour it resembles most cave forms in being pale pink. It seems certain that *A. jordani* evolved from a population of surface-living *Astynax* which had become trapped in a cave but had found sufficient food to survive. Thereafter they became adapted to cave life. This is probably the only cave fish that the aquarist is likely to purchase, most others being extremely rare. It is a hardy fish which does not require darkness and seems to compete well in a community tank. It grows to about 3 in (7·5 cm) and is constantly on the move.

The members of the genus *Copeina* from South America bear a superficial resemblance to the egg-laying toothcarps and they lack the adipose fin. *Copeina arnoldi* has interesting breeding habits. A pair of fish will move into shallow water where there is plenty of overhanging leaves 1–2 in (3–5 cm) above the surface of the water. The male and female then leap out of the water and adhere belly uppermost to the underside of a leaf. A few eggs are laid and fertilized and the fishes drop back into the water. This process is

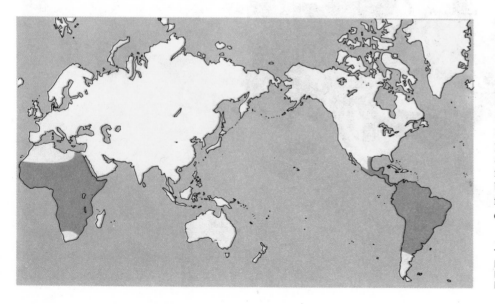

The distribution of the Characinidae or characin-like fishes. Note the absence of characins from North America, Europe, Asia, Australasia and Madagascar.

Most characins are carnivores, but *Myleus* sp, shown here, a relative of the fierce piranha, eats only plants and is quite inoffensive.

repeated time after time until all the eggs are laid. The male then stays below the eggs and splashes water onto them with his tail to keep them moist until they hatch about 36 hours later. Other members of this genus lay their eggs on large-leafed water plants or in pits in the sand. The male cleans the site before the spawning and fans the eggs after they are laid in much the same way as some of the cichlid fishes.

The genera *Hemigrammus* and *Hyphessobrycon* contain most of the small and pretty characins popularly referred to as tetras. There are, however, several other genera that also contain species commonly known as tetras. Recent work on the classification of these fishes may result in some changes in the scientific names but the names used here are so entrenched in the literature that they can easily be traced if more information is required. The tetras are lively but peaceful shoaling fishes with an upstanding small dorsal fin. Many can be easily bred in aquaria and there are a number of good popular books devoted to the care of these fishes. To show their colours best, they need

a certain amount of room, clumps of plants for shade, several companions of their own species, and slightly acid, peaty water. Only a few of the many species can be described here.

The Glowlight tetra *Hemigrammus erythrozonus* has a grey-green body with a glowing ruby-red stripe along it and touches of red and cream on the transparent fins. It grows to about 2 in (5 cm) and comes from Guyana. The Flame tetra *Hyphessobrycon flammeus* has a red body with two vertical dark bars and is found near Rio de Janeiro. The Neon tetra *Hyphessobrycon innesi,* probably the best known of all, was named after William Innes who has done so much to inform aquarists about fish and how to care for them. It has an iridescent green stripe from the eye to just below the adipose fin and beneath this, from the chest to the tail, is a gleaming red stripe. The Cardinal tetra *Cheirodon axelrodi,* from forest pools in the upper parts of the Rio Negro, has the same colours as the Neon tetra but both bands run the full length of the body. The Beacon fish *Hemigrammus ocellifer* has an

olive-green or brown body with an orange spot at the base of the tail and another on the shoulder. It is an easy fish to breed in captivity. The Serpae tetra *Hyphessobrycon serpae* is rather variable in colour and several species names have been given on the basis of different colour varieties because, as so often happens, little or no information can be found of the place of origin of specimens sold by dealers. It has been suggested that the Serpae tetra, the Rosy tetra *H. rosaceus,* the Deep-red tetra *H. minor* and some others are in fact all colour varieties of the single species *H. callistus.* To the aquarist such difficulties with the scientific names may seem unimportant until it is realized that unless the names truly reflect the relationships of the various forms, data on habits and breeding possibilities are liable to be misleading. Also included in the general term tetra is the Platinum tetra *Gephyrocharax atracaudatus,* an elongated vividly silver species from Panama.

It is true to say that the African characoids in general are less colourful than their South American relatives. The Congo tetra

Micralestes interruptus, however, is one of several exceptions. It has an elongated, compressed body which reflects a multitude of colours in irregular patterns. The central rays of the tail in the male are prolonged into a 'sword-tail', the gill cover is a metallic green and there is a bright blue spot behind it. The body is brown to gold along the back and below this there is a red-brown stripe followed by a greenish line and below this again a bright green line, while the belly is often violet.

Another characoid family, the Anastomidae, includes the headstander *Abramites microcephalus,* a stocky little fish with a small and pointed head that spends most of its time with its body pointing vertically downwards. Several other anastomids, such as the Spotted headstander *Chilodus punctatus* have the same habit. These fishes feed off the bottom, scraping algae or small organisms off the rocks.

The family Curimatidae contains softmouthed characoids that go into estuaries. Dr E. Herald has commented on the resemblance between the habits and mouths of these fishes and those of the Grey mullets of European coasts.

The South American family Hemiodontidae (meaning half-toothed, a reference to the absence of teeth in the lower jaw) contains active, silvery fishes, some of which, for example *Characidium fasciatum,* swim with peculiar jerky movements.

The family Lebiasinidae includes the pencilfishes, discussed elsewhere. A separate article is also devoted to the hatchetfishes of the family Gasteropelecidae.

In Africa there are two families of deep-bodied characoids. In the Distichodontidae, from the Congo basin, the adipose fin and part of the tail are covered with scales. These are active fishes found mainly in the deeper parts of rivers. In *Distichodus affinis* the tail is formed of two separate lobes almost completely covered by scales, which gives a

Blind cave characin of Mexico.

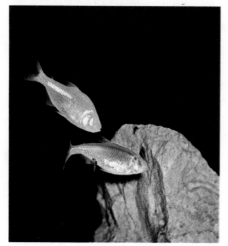

Cardinal tetra is distinguished from its relatives by the red band over the full length of the body.

rather curious appearance to the fish. It is a fairly large species, growing to 2 ft (60 cm) in length and is an important food fish. Members of the other family, Citharinidae, are also very deep-bodied and somewhat resemble the South American *Metynnis* or 'vegetarian pirhana'. These fishes are found in some of the African lakes and are again important food fishes.

Africa also has its pike-like characoids, for example species of the genus *Phago* from the Niger basin. These are elongated, cylindrical fishes with long snouts and well armed jaws. The scales are large, with only about seven vertical rows on the body and in addition are rough-edged or ctenoid, a type of scale usually found in the more advanced perch-like fishes.

The characoid fishes are clearly a highly successful group. The large number of species and the diversity of forms found in South America as compared to Africa may perhaps reflect the fact that they have not had to compete for food and living space in South America with the equally successful carp-like fishes of Africa and other parts of the world. ORDER: Cypriniformes, CLASS: Pisces.

CHATS, certain species of birds of the thrush family. Turdidae, in the Old World; the American wood warbler family, Paluridae, in the New World; and the Australian wren subfamily, Malurinae, family Muscicapidae. The name derives from the 'chatting' call notes of many of the species, including the whinchats and stonechats, *Saxicola* spp, the wheatears, *Oenanthe* spp and the redstarts *Phoenicurus* spp. ORDER: Passeriformes, CLASS: Aves.

CHEQUERED BEETLES, predacious insects so named because their bodies often bear checkered markings of various colours. These are attractive little beetles with cylindrical, hairy bodies. They are sometimes encountered on flower heads, in clumps of moss or, more frequently, under bark. The family is fairly large, with some 2,500 species. By virtue of their predacious habits, they are sometimes useful biological control agents, checking the populations of injurious plant-feeding insects such as Bark beetles. Some Chequered beetles are scavengers and a few live in bees' nests. FAMILY: Cleridae, ORDER: Coleoptera, CLASS: Insecta, PHYLUM: Arthropoda.

CHEECHAK *Hemidactylus frenatus,* or Common house gecko. It gets its name from the call it makes when prowling about at night for food. It prefers native huts and some city buildings as its habitat. Its origin was mainland Asia, but by hitching a ride on boats and in cargo, it has spread to most of the Pacific Islands. In the daytime, the cheechak is dark brown to nearly black as it hides in crevices. At night, when on the prowl, it becomes almost ghostly white. FAMILY: Gekkonidae, ORDER: Squamata, CLASS: Reptilia.

CHEESE MITES, tiny animals related to spiders, living on cheese, its high content of fat and protein, and the moulds, on ripe cheese, being attractive to mites, which are detritus feeders. Cheese mites belong mainly to three genera, *Tyrophagus, Glycyphagus* and *Acarus.* The *Glycyphagus* are particularly partial to moulds, but by far the most common mite found on cheese, in Britain at least, is *Acarus siro,* the Grain mite.

Since mites are small, they usually escape notice until large populations have built up and the surface of the cheese has become covered with a fine dust of cast skins, excreta and dead mites; it will also be surrounded by a ring of this dust. That the dust contains live mites is easily shown: a small conical heap of such dust will spread out in the course of a few minutes at room temperature. In cheese stores, the mites are dispersed by crawling from cheese to cheese. Softer cheeses are more liable to infection than hard ones. The mites are controlled, to some extent, by the oiling of the cheese at intervals during the ripening process to produce a hard leathery surface and, in the case of Dutch cheeses, by a final coating of wax; these cheeses were at one time covered with an envelope of pig's bladder. Heavy infestation of cheese and penetration into the interior causes great wastage. Farmhouse cheese in France and Germany may be infected deliberately to give it bouquet and a particular appearance. ORDER: Acari, CLASS: Arachnida, PHYLUM: Arthropoda. T.E.H.

CHEETAH *Acinonyx jubatus,* the 'odd man out' of the family Felidae, it shows many dog-like characteristics that are not to be found in the other cats. It has long legs and is built for great turns of speed, from which it gets the reputation of being the fastest mammal in the world. The feet are of a very similar construction to the dog, in that they have hard pads with sharp edges, rather than the soft elastic pads that are found in the rest of the cats. These pads, and the blunt, non-retractile claws have a definite purpose in giving this very fast moving animal the additional grip required for sudden stops and turns. The dew claws are worthy of note as they are more developed than in the other cats, and they play a big part in gripping prey. The head is small in comparison to the rest of the body and the eyes are set high upon it which helps the animal when peering over low cover and hillocks. The ears are small and rather flattened, reducing the silhouette still further. The nasal passages are larger than in the other cats to allow the intake of the extra oxygen required for the final sprint to the prey.

The cheetah is easily distinguished from the other cats, not only by its loose and rangy build, but also by the very distinctive markings. The ground colour of the coat is a reddish shade of yellow and is broken by spots of solid black. The face is marked by the very noticeable 'tear stripes' running from the corner of the eyes down the sides of the nose. There is another form, called the King cheetah, which has been given the suffix of 'rex' but this appears to be no more than a recurrent mutation. The male measures 7 ft (2·1 m) overall, of which the tail, a very effective aid to turning, measures 2½ ft (0·8 m). The height at the shoulder is

Cheetah, the unusual cat that runs its prey down instead of stalking it.

Cheetahs usually hunt singly and for medium-sized prey but combine to seize a larger quarry.

about 2 ft 9 in (0·83 m) and the total weight of the animal is about 130 lb (59 kg). The female is usually about three quarters of the size and weight of the male.

Cheetahs are distributed from Algeria and Morocco to the Transvaal, through Egypt, Ethiopia, Arabia, Syria, Persia and India, and throughout much of its range it has been captured and trained as a hunting leopard, which is one of its names. When it is trained, it is used in very much the same way as a coursing greyhound. The only fossil remains are in Asia and this suggests that this animal has migrated to Africa, probably through its association with man, although it is now more common in Africa than in Asia. In the wild, the cheetah will hunt either with a partner, or as a member of a group and it lives mainly on the smaller antelopes or the young of some of the larger species, although it has been observed taking quite small mammals. When the kill has been made, the cheetah prefers to eat the heart and kidneys first, and it also drinks the blood. After that the head is eaten and only then is the muscle meat attacked. It is not usual for a cheetah to return to a kill after the first feed. This difference in feeding habits is reflected in the teeth which are neither as large, nor as sharp as those of the leopard.

There appears to be no regular breeding season, and two to four kittens may arrive at any time of the year. At birth, the coat is a blue grey colour on the back and the rest of the animal is brown with dark spots. The young are born blind and the eyes open after about two weeks. The kittens, unlike the adult animals, are good climbers, and this fact, combined with other points of specialization suggests that these are cats that are developing away from the general cat type.

The African race *Acinonyx jubatus jubatus* is still fairly plentiful, although it is not as widespread as it used to be, but the Asian race *Acinonyx jubatus venaticus* is now listed as decreasing and in danger of extinction. FAMILY: Felidae, ORDER: Carnivora, CLASS: Mammalia.   N.J.C.

CHEETAH SPRINTS. The cheetah is credited with being the fastest land animal but it is very difficult to determine its maximum speed accurately. This is mainly due to the characteristic that the cheetah shares with other cats of being a sprinter. Prey is caught after a short burst of speed and, if the prey eludes capture, the cheetah gives up. Dogs, on the other hand, are long distance runners and relentlessly run their prey down. There are two records of cheetahs attaining 71 mph (114 kph). On one occasion a cheetah covered 700 yd (640 m) in 20 sec, timed by a stopwatch, and a second covered 80 yd (73 m) in $2\frac{1}{4}$ sec.

CHEIROLEPIS, one of the earliest known genera of actinopterygian fishes. Two species have been described: *Cheirolepis trailli* from

the Middle Devonian of Scotland and *Cheirolepis canadensis* from the Upper Devonian of Canada. An unusual feature of this genus is the covering of very small, diamond-shaped scales unlike those of other actinopterygians but similar to the scales of acanthodians. SUBCLASS: Actinopterygii, CLASS: Pisces.

CHELONIA, name of the order which includes tortoises, turtles and terrapins, now replaced by the order *Testudines.

CHEVROTAINS, tiny deer-like animals, the smallest of all artiodactyls or cloven-hoofed animals being only about 1 ft (30 cm) high at the shoulder. They have a small head, pointed snout and long, remarkably thin legs. The coat is of very short hair, usually a warm brown marked with various white stripes and spots, though some plain forms do occur. The underside is usually white.

They are often called Mouse deer because of their small size but, despite their superficial resemblance to deer, chevrotains are probably more closely related to pigs and camels. They have neither horns nor antlers and

Chevrotains or Mouse deer.

although they are ruminants the stomach is much simpler than in the true deer. Chevrotains also lack the typical scent glands on the face or legs seen in deer. A similarity with the pigs, and to a lesser extent camels, is seen in the upper canines, which are long, curved and sharp, especially in the male, and project downwards outside the lower lip. Perhaps these are used by the males for fighting as well as for defence. The cheekteeth form a long series ideally suited to grinding the leaves and fruit upon which the animals feed. As in other artiodactyls the feet have the middle two toes greatly enlarged and the animal's weight is borne mainly on these. In chevrotains the two lateral toes are also quite well developed and may actually touch the ground in walking. This is a primitive condition and represents an early stage in the evolution of the two-toed foot seen in deer, where the two lateral toes are vestigial.

The Water chevrotain *Hyemoschus aquaticus* lives in the dense forests of West and Central Africa, the several species of *Tragulus,* including *T. javanicus,* the most common, and the meminna *T. meminna,* inhabit the similar tropical habitat of India and Southeast Asia. All chevrotains live almost invariably near rivers and swamps, threading their way carefully through the dense vegetation, mainly at night. They are solitary, very shy and consequently rarely seen except for a fleeting glimpse of one crouching low and vanishing swiftly into the undergrowth. The females give birth to one or sometimes two young after a gestation period of four months.

Though seldom seen, chevrotains are quite common and form an important item in the diet of various predators including the carnivores, snakes and men who live in the forest. FAMILY: Tragulidae, ORDER: Artiodactyla, CLASS: Mammalia.   P.A.M.

CHICKADEE, the American name for some seven species of the genus *Parus,* which in Europe are known as *titmice. About four more species of *Parus* occur in North America, which in contrast to the chickadees have crests and are called titmice in America. FAMILY: Paridae, ORDER: Passeriformes, CLASS: Aves.

CHICKEN, the term usually used for the young of the domestic fowl. See Fowl, domestic.

CHIGGER, the common name for the larvae of Harvest mites belonging to the family Trombiculidae. Also called 'redbugs' because of their colour, these parasites attach to the skin of birds and mammals and are often serious pests of man in rural areas, causing severe skin irritation or dermatitis. The rickettsial disease Oriental scrub typhus is transmitted by a Chigger mite.

The term 'chigger', sometimes written 'jigger' or 'chigoe' is also applied to a species of flea *Tunga penetrans.* See Harvest mite and flea. FAMILY: Trombiculidae, ORDER: Prostigmata, CLASS: Arachnida, PHYLUM: Arthropoda.

CHIMAERAS or ratfishes (sometimes also called rabbitfishes), members of a subclass of cartilaginous fishes related to sharks and termed the Bradyodonti (or Holocephali). The chimaeras are characterized by the presence of a curious appendage or 'clasper' on the head in front of the eyes. It is found only in the males, which suggests that it may serve some function in copulation. Like sharks, these fishes have a skeleton of cartilage and the males have one pair of claspers or more modified from the pelvic fins which are used for internal fertilization. They differ from sharks, however, in that the gill openings are covered by an operculum (resembling the gill cover of bony fishes) the primary upper jaw elements are fused to the skull (free from the skull in sharks but fused

Male chimaera *Chimaera monstrosa,* front view and side view, and (top right) upper part of head enlarged showing clasper and lateral line canals.

in the lungfishes); the anus does not discharge into a *cloaca together with the urinary and genital products but has a distinct opening of its own (as in the bony fishes). Highly characteristic are the teeth of chimaeras, which are formed of three pairs of large flat plates, two above and one below, armed with hard points or 'tritors' in some species but remaining beak-like in others. The majority of species belong to the genera *Chimaera* and *Hydrolagus* in which the snout is fairly blunt, the mouth ventral, the tail elongated and rat-like, and the first dorsal fin provided with a serrated spine capable of injecting a painful venom into wounds. *Chimaera monstrosa* is found along European shores and in the Mediterranean and grows to a length of 5 ft (1·5 m). Its scientific name aptly recalls the chimaera of Greek myth, one of Echidne's dreadful brood, a fire-breathing goat with a lion's head and a serpent's body which was finally slain by Bellerophon. Members of the genera *Harriotta* and *Rhinochimaera,* placed in a separate family Rhinochimaeridae, have a long pointed snout and only a single pair of claspers (there are two or three pairs in other species). Members of this family are found in both the Atlantic and the Indo-Pacific region and occur at depths of about 2,000–8,500 ft (600–2,550 m). The most monstrous of all the chimaeras are the members of the genus *Callorhinchus* (family Callorhinchidae) in which the snout is not only long but curls down and back towards the mouth. They are found in the cold and temperate waters of the southern hemisphere at depths of about 600 ft (180 m) off the coasts of South Africa, South America and Australasia but they also enter shallow water. They grow to about $3\frac{1}{2}$ ft (just over 1 m) in length. The earliest known members of this subclass were found in deposits of the Devonian period and are chiefly recognized by their highly characteristic tooth plates. The 20 or so modern

species are the survivors of a once widespread and successful group. FAMILIES: Chimaeridae, Rhinochimaeridae, Callorhinchidae, ORDER: Chimaeriformes, SUBCLASS: Bradyodonti, CLASS: Chondrichthyes.

CHIMPANZEE *Pan troglodytes,* the smaller of the two African apes and, with the gorilla, the species closest to man. Generally placed in the family Pongidae together with the gorilla, orang-utan and gibbon; but sometimes separated from the Asiatic apes and removed along with the gorilla to the Hominidae. Adult chimpanzees weigh 80–110 lb (36–50 kg); males are somewhat larger than females. The long, rather sparse hair is black and the skin changes from flesh-colour in juveniles to bronze then black in adults. The face is long and prognathous and the lips thin and mobile. The brow ridges are marked and the ears are very large, often remaining light coloured long after the face has gone black. Although the basic locomotor pattern of the Pongidae is for brachiation (arm-swinging) and the chimpanzee's anatomy shows that it is descended from true brachiators (long arms, broad chest, short thumb, no tail), chimpanzees do little brachiating today; for nearly half their time is spent on the ground, walking quadrupedally on the backs of their knuckles, and when they go into the trees they climb and move with all four limbs equally, as often as swinging from their arms alone.

Chimpanzees are found throughout the African lowland forest belt, from Senegal in the west around the coast via Gambia, Portuguese Guinea, Guinea Republic, Sierra Leone, Liberia, Ivory Coast and Ghana. Here there is a break in the forest but chimpanzees may occur in the forest-savannah mosaic and orchard bush of Togo and Dahomey. In southern Nigeria chimpanzees are found and continue where the forest

Chimpanzees can use their hands for manipulative work even to the point of showing a primitive ability as artists.

broadens out and goes inland via Cameroun, Equatorial Guinea, Gabon, Cabinda, Central African Republic, Congo (Brazzaville), Congo (Kinshasa), the southern-most Sudan, western Uganda, Rwanda, Burundi and northwestern Tanzania. They ascend mountains to quite high altitudes, reaching 7,000 ft (2,100 m) in the Itombwe Mts (Congo) and 11,000 ft (3,300 m) on Mt Ruwenzori. Gorillas are more common at high altitudes, hence it is only on Ruwenzori, where there are no gorillas, that chimpanzees reach very high altitudes. They are found equally in forest outliers and in Guinea they have been observed right out on the savannah. As Adriaan Kortlandt has pointed out, it is likely that chimpanzees were more eurytopic (occupying a wide variety of habitats) before man's competition forced them to restrict themselves to the forest.

Throughout their wide range, there is only one species of chimpanzee, *Pan troglodytes,* but there are four well-marked subspecies, or geographic variants, which differ in size, colour, head shape and development.

The westernmost race is known as the Masked chimpanzee *Pan troglodytes verus.* The young of this race have a pale, flesh-coloured face with darker, bluish colouration around the eyes and across the bridge of the nose—hence the name. The hair on the head is neatly parted in the middle. As it grows older, the Masked chimpanzee gets darker-skinned, rather blotchily, and finally becomes a matt black, though the 'mask' is always visible; the ears never turn quite black, but remain bronze-coloured. The adult male develops a white beard, and both sexes turn bald, the male beginning with a triangular bald spot on the forehead, the female in a straight line backwards. Masked chimpanzees occur from the extreme west of the species range, across the 'Dahomey gap' in the forest, to the west bank of the lower Niger River.

From the east bank of the lower Niger, as far east as the Ubangui River and as far south as the lower Congo River, is found the Black-faced chimpanzee or tschego *Pan troglodytes troglodytes.* This race has not much trace of a parting when young and no 'mask', the face being all flesh-coloured with numerous large tan spots, like freckles. With age, these fuse and so the face turns first brown, then jet black, a much deeper and more shining black than in the Masked race; even the ears are black. There is no beard in this race, and both sexes sometimes become completely bald. Some individuals have an exceptionally broad nose rather like a gorilla's.

Along the north bank of the River Congo, and out to the eastern boundary of the species, is found the Long-haired or Schweinfurth's chimpanzee *Pan troglodytes schweinfurthii.* The young are flesh-coloured, as usual, and darken evenly to a matt black; the body hair is long and almost shaggy, and there are long cheek-whiskers. Males develop a white beard round the chops. They do not go bald as other races. Males in this species are much larger than females; in other races the disparity is not so great.

Finally, south of the River Congo lives the Pygmy chimpanzee *Pan troglodytes paniscus,* sometimes considered to be a distinct species. It is small-sized, about $\frac{4}{5}$ the height of the other species (about 3 ft/1m tall), but only half the weight, being very slenderly built. It has a rounded skull and small face, long cheek-whiskers, scruffy hair and rather small ears. The face is black almost from birth, except for the lips which remain flesh-coloured. All chimpanzees have a little white tuft on the rump during infancy, but the Pygmy chimpanzee keeps this throughout life.

Pygmy chimpanzees seem to be more intelligent than large ones. Robert Yerkes, the American psychologist, had one called 'Prince Chim' who was the most intelligent of all his apes. Whereas large chimpanzees hoot rather deeply and hoarsely, the Pygmy chimpanzee's call is more like a shriek, a high 'hi-hi-hi' rather than 'hoo-hoo-hoo'. It has been noticed that generally large races of chimpanzees copulate from the rear, 'more canum', but Pygmy chimpanzees mate from the front, 'more hominum'; however this is not an absolute difference, for like man all chimpanzees can copulate either way.

Chimpanzees are highly promiscuous. Females in oestrus develop huge pink genital swellings which serve as signals to males; a female at the height of oestrus may be served by half a dozen males in fairly rapid succession. The female's sexual cycle lasts 35 days; gestation is 225 days. Females in oestrus often leave the nursery group, even if they have infants, and join a bisexual band where they will mate.

An infant chimpanzee is carried on its mother's belly at first, clinging tight—a reflex which is well-developed from birth. Sometimes she places the infant on her back and will give it food when it reaches out for some. While she is busy feeding or making her nest for the night, she may 'hang up' her infant on a branch beside her. Infants scream and have temper tantrums, but generally they are ignored: indeed the whole band of chimpanzees carries on with its activities as if the youngster was not there. Mothers and their infants continue to associate even after the young have become independent, and up to a year after the birth of a second infant. The juveniles continue to build their nests near the mother's but at this stage they are associating more with their peers, playing amongst themselves—wrestling, chasing and swinging around: as they play they make little panting noises . . . laughter?

On the ground chimpanzees usually walk quadrupedally, using both hands and feet.

Chimpanzees spend half their time in trees in which they make themselves simple nests to spend the night. Infants sleep with their mothers.

Chimpanzees feed mainly on fruit, but also eat leaves, nuts, bark, ants, termites and even meat. They have been observed co-operatively stalking and killing prey, such as Colobus monkeys or young antelope, killing the prey by swinging it high and slamming it on the ground. This seems to be a 'cultural' variation, however, and has only been recorded in chimpanzees living in rather open woodland.

Chimpanzees live in large societies of as many as 60 or 80 individuals, occupying a home range of 8 sq miles (20 km²) in the rich Budongo forest (Uganda), but this will be much larger in less hospitable environments. Population densities vary from 2·6 per sq mile (Gome Stream Reserve, Tanzania) to 10 per sq mile (2·7 km²) (Budongo forest). The whole society does not stick together, however, but splits up into smaller bands of varying size during daily movement; indeed the whole local population rarely comes together. During the day, chimpanzees go around in four types of association: adult bisexual bands, all-male bands, 'nursery groups' (females with their young) and mixed bands. Males sometimes move around on their own. The general pattern is that the bisexual and all-male bands move around the home range seeking sources of food, such as ripe fruiting trees, while the nursery group stays in one place. The discovery by one of the wandering bands of a prolific food source is announced with hooting, screaming and drumming on trees, bringing other members of the local group to the spot.

Six to eight hours a day are spent foraging, the animals moving around the forest from one fruit tree to another. They may eat it on the spot or they may carry off food, sometimes running along the ground biped-ally with both hands full. At times when there is a sudden abundance of insects, such as termites, the chimpanzees spend a long time feeding on them. At other times they will break off a twig or grass stem, removing the side twigs to straighten it, and push it into a termite mound; termites crawl all over it, and the chimp then pulls it out and eats the termites. The same technique is used by forest chimpanzees to get honey from ground nests of wild bees.

The travelling band walks through the trees fairly slowly, well spaced out; generally the animals come down from one tree to get into another, very rarely jumping across. Occasional leaps have been seen but these are usually more of a drop, sometimes for as much as 30 ft (10 m). During heavy rain, they shelter under trees, huddled up. They jump across small streams or walk over the water on fallen branches, disliking to get their feet wet.

At night chimpanzees make themselves nests in the trees wherever they happen to be, not returning to any special area or to other members of the local group. These nests are made by bringing together, interlacing and patting down branches to make a platform with a rim, in which the chimpanzee lies with his legs drawn up and goes to sleep. The nests take only one to five minutes to make; usually a new one is made each night, but an old one may be reoccupied sometimes. All adults and youngsters over about three years of age make separate nests, but an infant sleeps with its mother. Nests are always built high in the trees. In the tall Budongo forest they are mostly between 20 and 60 ft (6–18 m) up. If two bands from different local groups have been feeding together, as sometimes happens, they move apart a little to make their nests.

In the early morning when a chimpanzee wakes up, he protrudes his rear end over the rim of the nest and defaecates, carefully avoiding soiling the nest. After this, he may go back to sleep, lazily pluck food if there is any within reach, or begin to get up.

Chimpanzees are thoroughly noisy animals: they call loudly throughout the day and even sometimes during the night. Their calls can carry up to two miles, and the drumming that accompanies it carries even farther. Calling occurs in numerous situations. When two groups meet, especially if there is a mature male in each, there is loud calling, increasing in intensity with the number of males in each group; not only calling, but drumming, shaking of branches and slapping the ground. When a group reaches a fruiting tree, it calls for ten minutes or more, and other bands respond by calling back and moving towards the source of the calls. Nesting, and waking up in the morning, are the occasions for vocal celebration, especially if a large group is nesting together; the splitting up of a big group is accompanied by calling; on moving on to a new area, a band will call and drum, and during their movements they will call, often for no apparent reason. There is occasionally an outburst of calling and drumming which lasts for hours, known in Cameroun as a 'carnival' or 'kanjo'. The carnival can take place by night as well as by day. Vernon and Frances Reynolds, who studied chimpanzees in Budongo, experienced six carnivals, four by day and two by night. In two cases, there seemed to be evidence that several unfamiliar bands, probably from different local areas, had met at a food source.

Within the local society there are no leaders and there is very little trace of the 'rank order' seen in monkey societies. But big males, especially old and greying ones, are dominant to other individuals and are given right of way, but they do not threaten or bully the others. Quarrels, which last only a few seconds and involve stamping and branch shaking as a kind of threat, often break out. Sudden attacks, never serious, may occur. Females are more excitable and quarrelsome during oestrus. When two individuals meet after a separation, there is some form of greeting ceremony between them: the subordinate animal will approach the dominant one, a male, and touch the top of his head, his shoulder, thigh, groin or genitals; two males may greet each other by standing up with one arm held high, one running towards the other. They then fling their arms round each other. During the greeting ceremony, males usually have erections. A form of greeting, without involving prior separation, is appeasement—a male will go up to his superior and touch his lips or scrotum, a female will 'present' (i.e. turn her genitalia towards him). Appeasement may precede the subordinate animal coming to sit down and feed beside the dominant one. A subordinate animal may occasionally beg for food from a more dominant one, with palm held up.

Chimpanzees constantly utilize natural objects for their own purposes. Not only do they catch termites with the aid of sticks, but they will also crumple up leaves to make a sponge to soak up water out of a hole in a tree, and use large sticks as weapons, either throwing them or actually rushing up to the enemy and giving it a resounding thwack. A large chimpanzee, when angrily jumping up and down, stick in hand and with all his hair standing on end, is a terrifying sight and a formidable foe. When carrying objects, either 'tools', weapons or food, chimpanzees will walk or run upright, for as much as 30 yds (28 m); otherwise their bipedalism is restricted to occasional acts, such as standing up to look over long grass.

Such is the chimpanzee's life in the wild: noisy, peaceful, friendly. In captivity, psychological tests have indicated a high level of intelligence, and experts have sometimes been puzzled why this should be so, since the species does not appear to use its exceptional mental powers much in the wild. However, these abilities are used on occasion, and it is easy to visualize times when they would be essential to the animal's survival. The co-operative stalking of prey has been mentioned. When faced with an aggressor, chimpanzees' defence also tends to be co-operative. Unlike gorillas, whose intelligence seems very comparable, chimpanzees

show great facility with inanimate objects and can discover for themselves how to use poles and other objects to obtain food, by knocking it down from the ceiling or drawing it into their cage. By contrast gorillas cannot grasp the technique of doing this even when shown the way. Wolfgang Koehler during the First World War had a colony of chimpanzees on the Canary Islands with which he carried out psychological experiments, which proved quite startling to the world at large. In particular, the feats of his male chimpanzee, 'Sultan', have never been equalled before or since. Sultan could fix two poles together to reach his food, or pile boxes on top of one another if one box was insufficient. However, he could not appreciate the law of gravity, and time after time the boxes would come crashing to the floor because they were not securely balanced and were upset when he clambered on them.

Chimpanzees feed mainly on fruit, but also eat leaves, nuts, bark, ants, termites and even meat.

However, as one might expect from the behaviour of chimpanzees in the wild, persistence is not a commmon feature of their behaviour during tests. In this the gorilla, with his painstaking methodical approach, comes out far ahead of the chimpanzee, and by sheer persistence will solve problems that any chimpanzee would have got bored with long before. Both species will tackle problems for their own sake, rather than just simply to get food, but the gorilla is the more apt to do this.

The chimpanzee and gorilla are more closely related to man than are any other animals; they share anatomical details with man that even the orang-utan does not. Behaviourally, too, they are similar to man;

in human society similarities can be seen to both the one-male polygamous or the monogamous units of the gorilla, and the large open society of the chimpanzee with its breadth of contacts and easy subgroup formation. Similarly, man possesses both the dedication and persistance of the gorilla when faced with a problem, and the lively mind and manipulative ability of the chimpanzee. Like gorillas and chimpanzees, man is terrestrial; the structure of the foot, hand and vertebral column of the two African apes foreshadows that of man to a much greater degree than does that of the orang-utan.

The evolution of man is well-known because man's way of life is a successful one, and was so from the moment he adopted it. However, the apes are as rare today as they were in the past (chimpanzees are the commonest apes but compared with most monkeys even they are scarce), and their remains have been few and far between since the end of the Miocene (11 million years ago). It is possible to see, however, that both chimpanzees and gorillas evolved from a type of ape *Proconsul* found in the African Miocene, and that man's ancestor *Ramapithecus* also came from this stock; whereas the orang-utan's ancestor *Sivapithecus* had already separated from this line and migrated into Asia. Consequently man, the gorilla and the chimpanzee evolved in Africa, and their ancestors began to become separate about 12 million years ago; the orang-utan's ancestors had separated about 16 million years ago.

The chimpanzee is a remarkable manlike primate, an attribute which should not be embarrassing but endearing, and it is essential that it should be preserved, both in the wild and in captivity, for posterity. FAMILY: Pongidae (or Hominidae), ORDER: Primates, CLASS: Mammalia.   C.P.G.

CHIMPANZEE FIRST AID. One of the most endearing stories about chimpanzees concerns the removal of a piece of grit or some other foreign body from the eye of a chimpanzee by its mate. The pair concerned were Pan and Wendy who had lived at the Yerkes Laboratories in Florida for some years. One day Pan was boisterously showing off to visitors when Wendy came up behind him, whimpering. Pan immediately turned towards and squatted in front of her, then proceeded to inspect her left eye, pulling the lower lid down with one finger. After a while the inspection concluded, apparently with the removal of a foreign body for Wendy lay down relaxed. Pan also seemed pleased with the job because he sat quietly by Wendy having given up his attempts to attract attention.